MW01711650

Pool of Wealth Presents

3 STEPS TO RICHE$

A guide to Wealth and Success for Everyday People

3 Steps to Riches
www.3stepstoriches.com

Ordering Information:
Quantity sales and special discounts are available on quantity purchases by corporations, associations, schools and others. For more details or if you have special orders by trade bookstores and wholesalers contact the publisher at the address above or email
info@poolofwealth.com .

Printed in Canada

First Printing, 2013

ISBN: **978-0-9918969-1-2**

FOREWORD

New York Times Top 10 Best-selling Author

For the last 20 years I have been one of the most sought-after speakers in North America on the topics of wealth and success. I am also a New York Times best-selling author of such books as "*Chicken Soup for the Parent's Soul*™"*&*"*Branding for Dummies*". *I have accumulated a great deal of wealth and success for myself and those I love and I can personally validate the teachings in 3 Steps to Riche$. One of my core beliefs is you must make transformational experiences for yourself if you want to become rich. Within the pages of this book are such tools required to take you from being interested in becoming rich to helping you dedicate yourself to actually accumulating real wealth. This book is perfect for:*

- *People looking to get promoted*
- *People looking to make more money*
- *People looking to start a new business*
- *People looking to find their life's purpose*
- *People not sure how to take an idea from conception to reality*

3 Steps to Riche$ breaks down many required tactics I have used to move from a place of mediocrity to becoming one of the top 3 percent earners in North America. My favorite step is step 2 which talks about taking your passion and creating a plan to get you from point A to point B. Will Roger said "Even if you're on the right track, you'll get run over if you just sit there." Your passion is the equivalent of your dreams and your dreams will remain a dream unless you turn it into an actionable goal. You must take action and move forward if you want to transform your life to one of abundance. Many people waste their days doing transactional activities like going to work, dreaming about things they want and maybe even taking courses on self improvement, but 3 Steps to Riche$ shows you how to make transformational activities which are life changing and put you in the direction to wealth and success.

I was honored to write this foreword as wealth accumulation really does boil down to finding your passion, having a plan to create a business model around that passion and setting up a strong support system to keep you on the right track. Duane has taken this time tested methods to success utilized by many millionaires today and makes the process accessible to the everyday person. 3 Steps to Riche$ is truly a need to have guide for anyone searching to accumulate wealth and success for themselves.

Raymond Aaron
– New York Times Best-Selling
author and motivational Speaker

TABLE OF CONTENTS

INTRODUCTION

Some theologians may condemn the premise of this book as it may lead people to put money above all other human needs which will lead to sin and corruption. Many say money is the root to all evil but I challenge that statement. I say it is the LOVE of money and/or the LACK of money which is the root to all evil. Money is but a tool which displays your heart's intent and the personality of your soul. If you are a selfish person without money, when you have money, that personality is enhanced. If you are a giving person, then when you have money, you will increase the amount of giving you share with the world.

In the Bible, God asks you to give to him your first fruits that you may prosper. Money is but a tool to help the needy, enrich those you love and assist you in living an abundant life. If your purpose is to become rich for entirely selfish reasons, this book is not for you. If you have a desire to use money as a source to improve the lives of those around you, to give back, to serve the universe and leave a legacy for your family - I urge you to read on and follow the steps outlined in the pages of this book

What is a Millionaire? Being a Millionaire is more of a mindset instead of monetary accumulation. Many people have accumulated millions of dollars but through various life experiences, they lose it, waste it or do not enjoy it. Everyone's lifestyle is a reflection of their true self image. Wealth can mean good health, good relationships as well as ability to purchase consumer goods. If you want to become wealthy, you must follow some, if not all, attitudes and behaviours of the rich. You must also utilize your God given creative faculties and take some sort of action. Action is always required - Action is the elixir for all riches.

In a world of fast answers, lack of patience and need for speedy resolutions, I wanted to write a book that shaved out the fluff and focused on the important aspects of becoming rich. Becoming rich is actually very easy once you understand what it takes to become rich. Being creatures of habit, the hard part is breaking old habits, beliefs and attitudes towards being rich. The hope is after reading this book, you will have the urge to continue reading titles with similar content and more in-depth tools and tactics to help realize your dreams and become truly rich.

I have studied numerous tried and tested get rich methods but, after taking the combined wisdom of people who have actually accumulated real wealth, I decided to write this condensed book to assist you on your journey. I am still on my personal journey to my desired level of riches, but through following the steps provided in the pages of this book, I have more than doubled my yearly salary in a few short years. I will continue to double my yearly income until I reach the level of income I desire. Today, I earn a well above average annual income, I travel at least three times a year and I am able to give monetary support back to the causes I believe in. I do not share these accomplishments to impress you but to impress upon you that YOU TOO can live a life filled with blessings. Prosperity is everyone's birthright. If you have taken the time to read this far, then I believe your heart is telling you there is something more for you in life.

Throughout the book, I will not only share aspects of my life's journey but I will provide information from experts I continue to learn from and still look to grow from their teachings. I have many mentors, some I know personally but most I have never met. Even so, it was through their direction that I have been able to identify my passion in life and share the tools for success I have cultivated over the years. It is not difficult to become rich. All that is required is a burning desire and determination to change your current situation and reach for greatness. The fire is in each and every one of us but it must be ignited and once that happens, life becomes magical. So, while you are reading, keep a pen handy so you can write down how you too can get in contact with some of my mentors. It costs you nothing to check them out and, in most cases, it does not cost you a penny for them to provide valuable information to assist you in your personal journey.

Lastly, I wanted to invite you to sign up for free to my website **www.poolofwealth.com** and be included in my daily motivational quotes from people throughout time who have provided uplifting words of encouragement and inspirational advice. At Pool of Wealth, you will also find links to some amazing programs from my mentors to help you on your journey to riches. At Pool of Wealth, we believe that procrastination can wait. Find your passion because prosperity is your birthright!

Before you begin, I want you to think about this fun Math formula on attitude I heard as a child:

<u>What equals **100%** in life?</u>

If: **A B C D E F G H I J K L M N O P Q R S T U V W X Y Z** Is represented as: **1 2 3 4 5 6 7 8 9 10 11 12 13 14 15 16 17 18 19 20 21 22 23 24 25 26**

Then: **H-A-R-D-W-O-R-K** = 8+1+18+4+23+15+18+11 = 98%

And: **K-N-O-W-L-E-D-G-E** = 11+14+15+23+12+5+4+7+ 5 = 96%

But: **A-T-T-I-T-U-D-E** = 1+20+20+9+20+ 21+4+5 = **100%**

The best way to read this book is with a positive attitude and understand the knowledge you learn is nothing without hard work. Without a positive attitude, however, you will not be able to give 100% in each of the 3 Steps to Riche$. I am excited about the ideas, creativity and innovation which will come at the hands of you, the reader. Get ready to change your life, get ready to change the world and get ready to become rich.

Duane Browne

Motivational Speaker and Success Coach

BECOMING RICH IS EASY!

"High achievers spot rich opportunities swiftly, make big decisions quickly and move into action immediately. Follow these principles and you can make your dreams come true."

Robert H. Schuller

Personal reflection: They say the fastest way to learn a language is to engulf yourself in country of that language. If all you see and hear is that language, your amazing brain is forced to alter its reality and learn the language in order to blend in and engage in activities. The same is true for those who truly have desire to become rich. If you spend most of your time with "workers" you will remain a worker. However, if you align yourself with bosses and owners of commerce; your opportunities for increase will increase. We all become whom we seek to be. Aligning can be as simple as understanding and prescribing to the traits, actions and behaviours common among the rich. The story below is how I changed my life from mediocrity to a passion driven lifestyle. I was always on an ongoing quest but my transition climaxed in the summer of 2002.

I use to frequent a friend's house and this house had an abundance of, let's call it, "extreme" social activities going on. Now, even though I did not engage in any of it, the mere fact I was there was an admission that I was ok with what was going on. In retrospect, there was nothing uplifting or beneficial to my professional or personal growth; it was only a place to pass time which was time well wasted. On one particular evening, I was there to hang out and what happened next forced me to make a hard decision to give my life purpose and not let my God given talents go to waste.

I was playing pool in the living room (yes there was a pool table in the middle of the living room). Then, there was a knock at the door. When the door opened, three men rushed in the house, tied everyone up with duct tape and demanded that we hand over any drugs and money that were in the house. Now, there were no drugs in the house and no one present had any affiliation with gangs, deviant activity or crime. However, weeks earlier, we discovered one of our so called friends was a dealer and substance addict. When we found out what he was doing, my friend asked him to not come around anymore. Even so, the damage was done. Outside eyes had already associated us with him and, since birds of a feather flock together, when he stole from them, it was as if we all stole. Being face to face with the potential of dying really puts your life into perspective. My feet and hands were tied up, I was punched a few times and this gun was pointed in my face while some stranger demanded drugs (about which I had no idea what he was talking). It is not until a person is brought face to face with their own mortality that they truly understand the value of their life. The interesting thing was during this altercation, all I could think about was my family and the shame they would have to deal with if I died like this. Would they think I was into drugs and crime? Would they think I was not who they thought I was? Even though I was not a part of that lifestyle, if I was to die, that would be the perception the world would get based on with whom I was associated. After what seemed like an eternity, the gunmen settled to steal our wallets, cell phones and small amounts of cash. We never saw our so called friend again and I never ventured back to that house, needless to say. Even though I did not do anything wrong or engage in any criminal activity, I was clearly a product of my environment and, in the eyes of the world, a part of that negativity.

Thinking back on that time, what could have been if I had surrounded myself with a real estate investor, business owner or community leader during that period? God was definitely speaking to me that even though I was on the path to riches, I had too many detours, too many self inflicted obstacles and too many unnecessary setbacks because I lacked focus (which gave rise to being prey to outside influences). Nothing wrong with having friends from different walks of life; but if you want to be rich, you must be conscious of the company you keep, how you spend your time and what you are willing to sacrifice to get what you want in life. I hope this book is your defining moment, the moment you make the decision edged in stone that you WILL become rich.

3 Simple steps

Becoming rich is really an easy exercise. It only involves 3 basic steps. There are many more steps to enhance your performance and results but the fastest and easiest path to riches involves three basic steps:

1. Identifying your passion
2. Setting clear goals to transform that passion to a monetary return
3. Creating your support system to assist in achieving those goals.

By following these three steps (in that order), you will be on your way to a life of success, wealth and riches. Some people have mastered finding their passion, some people have mastered being able to set planned out goals and others have an amazing support system in place. Until all three are combined, you will most likely fall short. You may be blessed to work in your field of passion, but unable to monetize it to a level where you can help others. You may have goals with a plan to get there but unless the goal is your true heart's desire, you will never be completely happy. You may have a strong support system but unless you know how to unleash the power of your network, you will never reach your God given net worth.

Personal reflections: Growing up, I was one of those kids who did not excel in school. It was not that I was not smart but I just did not have any motivation to excel. I had no desire to study, but focused my energies on participating in sports and playing with friends. My sister, on the other hand, was the complete opposite. She got straight A's and always seemed to do and say all the right things. So if two kids grew up in the same house, why was it that one child was a straight A student and the other was a D student? Both our parents wanted us to do well in school and we both had the same opportunities in life. We both had to do our homework before we were allowed to watch television and we even both attended the same after-school programs to give us "a leg up" in class.

The difference is one word - **Passion.**

My sister (her name is Abigail by the way) had a passion for education at an early age. She enjoyed soaking up information, getting data and presenting her results. She had a passion for learning. She thrived at being the best at information gathering and sharing information. It only makes sense that today she has two degrees and a Master's in Law. I, on the other hand, had no passion. Let me correct that: I had many passions but was yet to identify and acknowledge my passions. I had a strong support system (my father and mother) but I had not identified my passion. Since I had not identified my passion, I was unable to formulate any plans to bring them to reality. I did well in almost all sports but no plan to take my talents to the next level; it was impossible to improve my skill level and options.

Today, one of my greatest regrets is not having an understanding of where my talent in baseball would have taken me. Even if I did not make it to the Majors, I could have gotten a scholarship to college or been involved in baseball in some form or fashion. One of my passions growing up was baseball; however, without identifying it and setting forth a plan to continue and excel in it, I went from being a kid with amazing natural talent, to a good player to average. I had a strong passion for baseball but I took that passion for granted and my natural abilities never had the opportunity to blossom. Furthermore, because my parents did not understand the value in sports, they were unable to provide the support I required to develop my abilities. Who knows? I could have received a free education via a baseball scholarship. Or I could have been drafted to play for the Toronto Blue Jays – who knows what could have been if I identified my passion for baseball and had a plan and support system in place to take my talents to higher places?

Who is this book for?

A lot of "get rich" authors talk about their rags to riches stories and, through those stories, many people are inspired to strive for the same rags to riches experience. These rages to riches stories show the perseverance and persistence that come from a dedicated goal of amassing great amounts of wealth, matched with a solid execution plan. The premise is always, "If someone like me can do it, then surely you can do it too". The problem with these rags to riches stories is it may appear to speak to the majority of the population hoping to become rich but it DOES NOT in reality. The reality is there are three types of people as it relates to becoming rich and the majority of them are not where you would think.

The first group are the "arrived" group. This is the group who are already wealthy and enjoying the benefits of having the resources to enhance the lives of their family and friends. They are the owners of commerce, those rich by inheritance, and those rich by chance or those who have executed a plan to success and are now enjoying the fruits of their labour. The topic of getting rich is not as important to them as increasing and maintaining their wealth.

Then, there is the "can't fail- let's go" group. This group is the "rags" who want to become rich group. They are at the end of their financial rope and their entire being is in "do or die" mode. They are 100% committed to their end goal and the topic of getting rich is of great importance to them. Their mentality is simple - there is nowhere to go but up; I must focus all my energies to the task at hand and I must do it NOW. The problem with this group is getting to understand which get rich vehicle best matches their personal interests and God given abilities. This is the group where the magic happens but tragically an extremely small percentage of society falls into this group. The "arrived" and "can't fail-let's go" groups are closely related to each other. They are merely opposite ends of the same journey.

Lastly, there is the "middle of the road" group. This group is where I think the majority of people are. They have the desire to become rich, they understand the logic in all the various methods to riches but yet they have not become or are even close to becoming rich. They appear stuck in their efforts to make real parts to Riches and yet they may seem to be on track; they are unable to acquire the levels of riches they hope for.

The problem with this group versus the other groups can be summed up by this self-reflective question: are you interested in riches or committed to becoming truly rich? Life may not be perfect but their basic life requirements of food, shelter, and clothing are not in any immediate danger. They may hate their job but it is putting food on the table so they feel obligated to continue with their day to day patterns. They have bought into society's programming of a mundane, routine living and subconscious acceptance of the role they play in society. This programming begins at childhood and follows the masses up to their death bed. From an early age, we are told to go to school, get good grades so we can get into a good college or university which will in the end get us a good job and provide stability. The problem is the education system was not build to help people achieve wealth. If you look at the history of education, you will discover it was built by Industry owners to cultivate productive workers. Now, by no means am I denouncing the importance of education, but it should be used as a tool to increase the value you bring to yourself and fellow man. It should not be a means to an end of being employed by someone else – making <u>them</u> rich.

This book is for any of the three groups above but will benefit one particular group the most. If you are in the first group, this book will help you get back to the basics of success and help you multiply your wealth. If you are in the second group, this book will help you focus in on your already burning desire and get you to where you need to be faster.

For the last group, this book was created mainly for you in mind.

You are the group of people who know there is a better life out there for them but are stuck in their comfort zone. This book will engage the masses of people who may be interested in becoming rich but they are too comfortable to take all the action steps required to achieve the levels of riches they want. On Being comfortable Charlie Gilkey said, "*The majority of people can't answer "yes" to both questions. They're either pushing their boundaries to the limits and hence are uncomfortable, or they've become comfortable and stopped pushing.*" Humans are creatures of expansion but we are also creatures of habit. In all of us there is a desire for greatness but when we become stuck in our day to day activities, we become complacent and luke warm in going the extra mile to achieve greatness. Another way of thinking about it is to consider yourself as a water molecule. – When heating up water, you have to keep pushing forward to allow the water to get hot. The magic starts to happen once you reach the boiling point. Once water transforms into steam, that is where the breakthrough happens and as we know, steam is what made modern day society move forward.

Everyone at some point has to decide which path to take. You can continue to be a Slave to society and do what everyone else is doing or be the Master of your own destiny and create Riches and help your family and friends. If you are reading this book, take a chance on yourself, stretch your imagination and start implementing your vision to become rich!

What does it mean to become Rich?

Have you ever sat in bed and wondered what it would be like to be rich? Ever ask what is the point to life? Have you ever asked yourself if this is all that life has to offer? Even though this book is about becoming rich, wealth does not have to mean monetary wealth. Money is but a tool to fulfill your dreams and desires. If you are able to achieve all the things that matter most to you, then you are truly already rich. Since money is a tool, it is my hope and desire to provide the steps to achieving riches so that you may use your wealth for the greater good of those around you.

Have you ever felt the urge to do something special? If you are any part human, and unless you have already found your purpose in life, this question will relate to you. What separates humans from wild animals is our gift of intuition, free will and our soul. Animals are programmed to act and behave in a certain manner in accordance to the laws of nature. Humans, on the other hand, are able to govern their actions or inactions with a sense of reasoning as to why they have made their decisions. What all creation on earth does share is the sense of expansion. This sense of expansion is the essence of understanding what your purpose is in life – The key to creating Riches! All animals procreate for purpose of expansion. All plants grow from a seed for the purpose of expansion. When you think about it, our everyday activities have expansion in mind (money, success, power, influence, acceptance and more stability). The problem with humans is since we have intuition, free will and a soul, we must find our own purpose in life without the aid of nature's programming. Some individuals have been blessed enough to stumble upon it, some have been environmentally conditioned for it and, sadly, some have yet to discover it. Once your purpose has been discovered and you mix in a plan to incorporate it into your life, you are well on the road to riches.

I have been blessed with the knowledge of what my purpose in life is. I have also been blessed with the opportunity to live out my life's purpose and assist others find their purpose. My life's primary purpose is to help people empower themselves to achieve their own life's calling – Through sharing my story and principles I have learned along the way. Your purpose in life might be to share a God given talent or taking a problem and figuring out a solution which will help thousands of people. Your purpose can also be as simple as being able to put a smile on someone's face. The beautiful thing about finding your life's purpose is the benefits that are created by it. My benefit was taking something I enjoyed and creating a wealthy lifestyle from it which, in turn, created my ultimate life's purpose – to help you. Confucious said, "Do the work you love doing and you will never have to work a day in your life again". When you do what you love, time flies, networks of like minded unions are created, people are drawn towards you and life starts to make sense and become in harmony with nature – Then, that is when the magic of becoming rich happens.

Being truly rich is not defined by the number of dollar bills in your pocket or in your bank account. Being rich is being able to help those you care about. Be it through assisting with education, providing others with that dream vacation or having the extra time to help solve their problems, money is a tool to help those in need. With that said, it is not the only tool. The real tool to helping those in need is helping them help themselves. Money can be used to fund education, provide temporary relief while they get back on their feet or it can be used to invest in their vision.

Being rich is also having the time to be with those you love. With riches comes the option to spend more time with them. Since money is a tool, you must become its master and not allow it to control you. Many CEOs have lots of money but spend little to no time with family. True wealth is being able to control your tools (money), and create an environment where you can spend more time with your loved ones. To control money does not mean to necessarily own it. I have a friend who owns a beautiful boat and anytime I like, I am able to use his boat at my leisure. Would you say the average person is able to take a boat out on the lake? I would say no. Even though I do not own a boat, I have the benefits of being a boat owner.

Lastly, being rich is the ability to wake up every day healthy and able to work at your life's purpose. Even though this is the last point on being rich, it is the most important. Through living your life's purpose, you drive multiple paths to becoming rich. Through acknowledging and acting on your purpose in life, you will be in a position to accumulate wealth beyond your imagination. Now, sceptics might say money is not everything or money is the root to all evil but that is their paradigm. Money is nothing more than a symbol and through it, you can help those you love (and humanity) if your heart is in the right place. The paradox of it all is this: It is simple to find your life's purpose but it is hard to find yourself! Until you shift your paradigm of complacency and comfort, you will never truly grow. David B. Bohl said, "*In self growth, when we say you're comfortable, what we really mean is that you're not growing. You're not stretching yourself. You're satisfied where you are, and not making any real effort to move forward out of that situation*". Once you are in your growth zone, people, situations appear in your life to assist you. What the masses call luck is nothing more than preparation matched with identification of the right opportunity (which is all around us). Getting rich is easy – The hard part is convincing people just how easy it is!

Can you become Rich too?

Anyone and I mean anyone, with an ounce of imagination, determination and a plan, can become rich. If you are saying, you do not have the education, start up money or influence to become rich, then your definition on the tools needed to become rich are flawed. I urge you to read the "*Science of getting rich*" by Wallace Wattles to understand that education, start up money, influence, or any other external factor come after you start from within. Riches start from the inside. You must become wealthy on the inside before you will be able to become rich on the outside. Understanding inner riches is the secret sauce to becoming rich.

Many people are held back from achieving the life they deserve because they do not understand inner wealth equals outer wealth. The problem is many people look at wealth with a monetary measuring stick. When you are truly rich, it will appear in all aspects of your life. Situations, people and ideas will start to flow to you and, as if through magic, outer riches will start to materialize. Society teaches people that if you want to get money, you have to get a job. This is embedded in our brains from birth and branded into our subconscious throughout life (unless you break the paradigm today). Dan Lok who is one of my mentors said, "*Passive income is not difficult, it is only different*". What Dan is saying is anyone can become rich, you just have to condition your mind to think differently than the masses do.

You must act differently from the masses and you must develop habits differently from the masses. It is not always an easy ask to reprogram years of conditioning but the first step is to have a desire to step out of the matrix. To start analyzing what you do today and what you should be doing differently to develop a brighter future for yourself and those you care about.

Prepare your mind for riches

Becoming rich is easy, the difficulty is taking your God given talent and/or interests and formulating a plan to execute and capitalize on them. We all have dreams and we all have spent some time day dreaming. The only difference between dreams and goals are the action steps taken to turn your dreams into reality.

You also have to develop the mindset of becoming rich even before you make your first dollar. Your thoughts and perceptions about money are an example of the mental programming given to you throughout your life. People feel they are in control of their thoughts but the real boss is the subconscious brain (which you do not control). A fun example of our mental programming and the power of the subconscious over your conscious are provided below. It might not work for some but the example should work for most people reading this book.

Step 1: Sit up straight in a high chair then focus on your right foot.

Step 2: Take your right foot and now move it up and down (fast). Your brain told your foot to move up and down, correct? Well, something as simple as that is actually pre-programmed by your brain (but you think you had conscious control of it but your subconscious brain executed the request from your conscious brain to move your leg. If you doubt me then watch this.

Step 3: Now move your right foot in a fast circle clockwise motion.

Step 4: While moving your right foot in a fast circle, draw in the air a number 6 with your right hand – Notice how you cannot do both? If you have full conscious control like you say you do, you should be able to do what you want; but, clearly, you can't – It's all programming

Your conscious brain fires neurons at a rate of 40 times per second. Compare this to the subconscious part of your brain which fires neurons at a rate of 40 million bits of info per second. If you want to become rich your conscious brain must be in harmony with your subconscious brain. *It is very possible via the concept of brain plasticity to change negative perceptions of becoming rich.*

Without turning this into a science text, below are some simple principles of how our brain works as it relates to riches. Bob Proctor and John Assaraf, who from my perspective have a superior understanding of aligning your conscious with your subconscious, speak in depth about the science of how our brains actually operate and shifting paradigms that fosters a healthy relationship with money. They also speak in depth on operating in harmony with the conscious and subconscious portions of the brain to craft your own reality as it relates to being rich. Below is a crash course on this topic.

Paradigms are a multitude of habits and beliefs we all have within us. These come from our external environment such as media, friends, family, elders and mentors. This is why children are considered a blank slate. They soak up all external information because there is no reference point to draw from. This is how our self-image is created. Then, there is genetic and environmental conditioning.

A paradigm controls our perceptions about everything and shapes our logic. A simple example is that someone of Caucasian decent is considered a "white" person in society. If you look at a Caucasian, they are not actually the colour white at all. What else do you subconsciously believe to be true that is actually not fact but merely a perception on reality that might not be true? Lastly, paradigms are the gate keeper to what is important in life. Think about why you have not attained the riches you know you deserve. Your answer is an indication of your paradigm on the matter. So, how do we change it?

Shifting your paradigms to one in tune with becoming rich allows your brain to work in harmony with your soul's desire. Your Mind is the conductor of your body and your body is but an instrument of your mind. Your mind is broken down into two parts – Conscious and subconscious. Conscious part can only accept or reject what comes to it. Declarative, knowledge based, and simple beliefs about money are stored here. It accounts for about 2% of your brains capacity. Believe it or not, this is where you want to focus your effort. Through brain plasticity, the mind can change paradigms by creating new neural pathways. This is accomplished by figuring out what you want and training your brain to achieve it. If you are looking for more information on how to do this, check out John Assaraf's program (at the end of the book).

The reason you focus on the conscious is that it becomes a reflection of the subconscious portion of your brain. It accepts everything as fact. This controls procedural, deep rooted habits, beliefs – essentially, it is the power centre of your brain. This is why people are products of their environment. The key to change can be summed up in one word – education. Not education in the traditional sense, but true education of what is needed to get to where you need to be. I heard Bob Proctor talk about education and it changed my perception of it. He said, education comes from the Latin word "Educo" which means to draw out from within. That means you take what is already inside of us and we bring it out.

Everything you have to become rich is within you.

You have to train, cultivate and maintain our natural abilities to create the riches you deserve in life. Change this area of your brain as it relates to money and you will be on your way to riches. As bob Proctor says you are truly born rich!

BECOMING RICH IS EVERYONE'S BIRTHRIGHT!

"Rich people think and focus on opportunities while poor people focus on obstacles."

Unknown

You were born rich

Becoming rich is not only about monetary fulfillment, it is also about being genuinely happy with everything around you. Everyone on earth is born happy! Unhappiness is a learned experience through negative interactions in life. Look at babies, the simplest things brings smiles and laughter to their face. They take pleasure in embracing their environment and finding beauty in everything. That is what we, as adults, need to do – get back to the basics of our natural selves. Once you learn to get back to a state of happiness, then transforming that energy into riches becomes easy. Right now, I might be coming off a bit "New Agish" but if you had an extra $5000/month in your pocket, would you be a little bit happier? Of course you would. We are all born with the ability to bring forth the richness that is us and convert it into a monetary equivalent or money.

One of my favourite speakers is Stuart Knight. He gives a perfect example of how happiness or unhappiness is a learned activity. Here is an excerpt from one of his newsletters I prescribe to, "*…let's say the sport of hockey was never invented. If that was the case people in Toronto wouldn't be unhappy when their team lost. It would be impossible since the game doesn't exist. But the game does exist, and with it comes the learned response of attaching emotions to wins or losses. For hardcore fans, when the Maple Leafs lose, they don't see it as a group of men successfully using wooden sticks to put a rubber disk into a metal frame surrounded by mesh more often than other men. They see it as an extension of their true selves. But the game of Hockey could have just as easily NOT been invented as the game WAS invented. So the happiness a person feels when their team doesn't win could have been invented just as easily as it could not have been invented. It's all invented! I guarantee you that the majority of unhappiness that a person* *experiences in a lifetime is invented. Not having the right car, not having a baby by a certain age or not having the perfect figure are examples of that. For every reason a person can think of to not be happy, I can offer fifty examples as to why they should. Sure there are real moments of sadness such as the loss of a relationship or the death of a loved one, but these should only account for a small percentage of time with respect to a person's entire lifeline. Unfortunately, too many people spend way more time being unhappy than they should, not knowing that they have the power to change it. You shouldn't fear being unhappy. You should fear letting yourself be unhappy."*

When you are in a state of happiness, it is extremely easy to convert that energy into riches. Webster's dictionary defines "happiness" as a state of well-being and contentment or a pleasurable or satisfying experience. "Riches" are defined as abundant and/or valuable possessions. When you focus on things that bring you joy and look for business opportunities that help facilitate that happiness, you will more likely increase your abundance and have more joy. This, then, translates into a state of genuine contentment or pleasure – The road to riches.

When you are doing what you love, you are more likely to do it more, give it your best and excel at it. That is another secret sauce to monetary riches. If you are not doing what you love, stop doing it, delegate it or learn to love it. The key to riches is loving what you do and doing what you love!

Don't wait, get rich now!

"I remember the moment my life changed, the moment I finally said, "I've had it! I know I'm much more than I'm demonstrating mentally, emotionally, and physically in my life". I made a decision in that moment

which was to alter my life forever. I decided to change virtually every aspect of my life. I decided I would never again settle for less than I can be." - Anthony Robbins

We were all born rich but as we progress through life, we depart from those natural blessing. Why not get back on track now? We all want to have the resources to help those we love and assist with projects for which we have a passion. So stop procrastinating and having excuses and get started now. I recently read a blog from Bronnie Ware chronicling what she remembered when she worked for years nursing people on their death beds. She observed that people's perspectives on life are magnified when they are faced with their own mortality. The emotions of denial, fear, anger, remorse and, eventually, acceptance were all steps in reaching a state of peace before they passed away. Bronnie compiled responses over time of some of the regrets they had or if time was reversed, what they would have done differently. The interesting, yet unfortunate theme, kept reoccurring

The most common regret of all was people had wished they had the courage to life a life true to themselves not the life those around them expected them to live.

When people are on their deathbed, they reflect on their life and it is sad that so many dreams and aspirations went unfulfilled. Many people have not accomplished a fraction of their dreams and goals; it was all because of their inaction and acceptance to not go after what they wanted. The problem is that the majority of people have become comfortable with the uncomfortable. People accept their surroundings instead of looking to expand their experiences. They become complacent with the status quo thinking this is what their life will be, only to realize in the end, there was so much more that could have been done.

Don't wait until the end to realize you could have had a fuller and inspired journey filled with riches.

The other main themes that surfaced were the wish to express their feelings and allowed themselves to be happier. We all deny ourselves the freedom of expressing our feelings and being truly happy at some point in our lives. Too many people continuously do this and over time it becomes part of a mediocre existence and they never reach their full potential. We are the masters of our own destiny. We cannot control the reactions of others but we can control our actions in relation to them. Being your true self does one of two things: It enhances the relationship or releases the unhealthy, unnatural relationship. Either way, you are better off being honest with yourself. Bill Cosby said he did not know the keys to success but the key to failure is trying to please everyone. Being rich is a choice. Don't stay stuck in old thinking patterns and negative habits and beliefs about money. Do not become complacent and comfortable with your current situation.

Stop pretending to others and to yourself that you are content.

We are creatures of advancement and there are so many resources you can add to the world and those around you. We are all a reservoir of creativity that can be translated into money. You just have to start now; be honest with yourself and your abilities and get started.

Bonnie goes on to state, *"It is very important to try and honor at least some of your dreams along the way. From the moment that you lose your health, it is too late. Health brings a freedom very few realize, until they no longer have it."* The time is now. The moment will never be perfect, start on your road to riches today. Experiencing a blessed life is truly a choice. It is not the responsibility of your family, peers or friends; it is your choice and your life. Make a conscious effort to change and watch the magic happen

Keys to prosperity

The two most important factors required to develop your plan to riches are knowing where you are and knowing where you are going. I heard Bob Proctor say that many of the "get Rich Gurus" focus on where they are going, instead of laying the groundwork to build momentum. Bob continued to mention that the foundation for change is having a solid acknowledgment of where you are and what your habits patterns look like. The combination of knowing where you are and where you need to be sounds simple enough. However, you will be surprised at the number of people who underestimate the significance of these factors in becoming rich.

Knowing where you are is the self reflection of where you are in life and identifying where you want to go.

Once you start to work on the change you seek, you will find your productivity will start to compound your effectiveness. What do you do without giving any conscious thought to? For me, I own a motorcycle and I do not give any conscious thought to changing gears, looking out for blind spots and riding the clutch when required. Questions to ask yourself while you work on the change you seek are; What time do you wake up or start activities? How much time a day do you work on improving yourself of business? How do you approach and react to obstacles habitually? What negative habits do you have that should be broken? What habits are controlling your life?

Once you identify where you are, you can then turn your energies on where you are going.

Personal Reflection: One of my habits that needed to be acknowledged and changed was my morning activities. I was not a morning person and once I did get up, I was usually scrambling to start my day on time. For years I would say I was just not a morning person and it was hard to wake up early. Sound familiar to anyone you know? It wasn't until I acknowledged this habit as not ideal for my success that I started to make a conscious effort to change it.

I started to commit myself to going to bed a little bit earlier and calming my mind, body and soul before bed. I dedicated about 10 minutes before bed to get into this state of mind. Then, I set my alarm clocks an hour early. Yes, I said alarm clocks. I needed that extra push so I had one alarm clock by my bedside table and the other alarm clock across the room. I wanted to make sure I got up. Then, once up, I took 10 minutes to again calm my mind, body and soul and prepare myself for the day. I would take 45 minutes on developing myself through reading inspirational or self development books, audios and videos. What started to happen in my life reminds me of one of my favourite Bob Proctor examples. Imagine a rocket ship getting ready for takeoff. Consider the countdown as your decision to take action in your life. At blast off, there is a lot happening: smoke, fire, loud sounds and a lot of commotion. This could be considered all your combined efforts to change your current situation. Even with all this action, notice the rocket ship does not go anywhere – yet. Then. in a blink of an eye, the rocket ship shoots up into the atmosphere. That is what happened to me. I began to see the results little by little but over time the compounded benefits were realized and I blasted off from where I started in life and headed to the stars.

This book provides 3 Steps to Riche$ but within those steps there are actually 3 keys to prosperity that are ingrained in the text which are vital to your success. You will have a better understanding of these crucial keys to riches when imbedded into the steps, but below are the shortened version

Key 1: Matching your habits and beliefs with your reality. Your life or your reality is direct feedback to what your beliefs and habits are. Even if you think you know what your beliefs and habits are, your reality is a reflection of what you truly believe inside. An example is people who believe it takes money to make money. Since they do not have money, it does not make sense to try to start a new business or get into investing. Their beliefs match their reality (which is inaction). The fact is you do not need money to make money. Paul Blacquiere actually shows you how to make in real estate with no money. By the way, I tried it out and it works (I made $1500 by using key words in a conversation).

Key 2: Internal self talk and external visual stimulants. When you have continuous affirmations and self motivating conversations with yourself, you start to see a glimpse of it in your material world. It is like a mental stamp of approval to keep going. Start small and break things down into chewable portions. Once you become your own internal coach and motivator, your body is the machine to execute your will.

Key 3: Movement -The power of upward and onward movement and implementation of baby steps. The best example is the rocket ship example from above. It is the combination of all the little efforts that builds momentum and propels people to greatness. What is important to remember is to get started and that it takes time to build the momentum. Then, it is the consistent steps in the right direction that you will find movement towards riches.

The power of creating a system

The next factor that allows anyone to become rich is being able to understand the power of creating a system to get you to the levels of wealth you deserve. The book, *As a Man Thinketh*, talks about the power of systems in relation to your success. "*System is the law by which everything - every organism, business, character, nation, or empire - is built. By adding cell to cell, department to department, thought by thought, law by law, and colony to colony in orderly sequence and classification, all things, concerns, and institutions grow in magnitude and evolve to completeness."*

Becoming rich is easy and YOU can become rich as long as you follow a system and stick to that system.

Those who have a system are the creators and preservers of their vision for acquiring wealth. Keep in mind you must have the will to constantly improve your system and value your mistakes and the mistakes of others. It is in the acknowledgment of mistakes that future success becomes more attainable. Thomas Edison was a man who used a system to document his mistakes and failure to learn how not to do invent the incandescent light bulb. He said through all his mistakes he learned there were 1000 ways to not create it - this led to the **1** way to invent it – It all came down to systems

That is what this book comes down to. It is providing you with a system via 3 simple steps that will get you on the path to prosperity. These concepts are based on proven methods from those who have amassed and retained great amounts of wealth. Even though only 3 steps are outlined, it is by no means a get rich quick process. You must take the time to dedicate yourself to follow the steps and concepts if you are to transform your life.

Think of the getting rich process like a car driving at night. You have a starting point and you know your end destination. Through following instructions to your end destination (becoming rich), the path will appear little by little. Your headlights can only show you the way bit by bit. You must continue forward and, as you drive forward, the journey becomes more evident. Becoming is the same way. Once you discover where you are today and where you would like to be tomorrow, the path to prosperity will appear bit by bit if you follow these 3 steps.

Some people say money is the root of all evil. I think this comes from those who have a negative idea of what money can do. I believe the lack of money is the root to evil. It is in this state of lack where the sin really takes place - it is that quest for more regardless of who it negativity impacts. Money is but a tool and expression of your heart. Your goal should be to get rich and use your resources to better the lives of those you love and care about.

So are you ready to become rich? Let's get started!

STEP 1
IDENTIFY YOUR PASSION

There is no passion to be found playing small - in settling for a life that is less than the one you are capable of living.

Nelson Mandela

INVEST IN YOUR MIND, BODY, & SOUL

Education is the investment our generation makes in the future.

Mitt Romney

Be honest with yourself

Personal story: I was never a great student in school. I was not stupid but nothing ever inspired me to try. I remember report card after report card of teachers saying if only I would apply myself, I would have better grades. In my mind, the only difference between good grades and bad grades was my parents saying "good job" or saying "Duane, you need to do better". I would say to myself what kind of incentive was that? Plus, even kids who had worse grades than me would still get to move to the next grade. Throughout most of my education, no one ever helped me to identify my passion and what I enjoyed.

Identifying your passion is the first step to riches

If you think you already know what your passion is, I challenge you to read on to help solidify or change your perception of a passion. If you do not know what your passion is, this chapter is dedicated to uncover, discover and cultivate your passion. Once you know what excites you, you are well on your way to becoming rich. When we are children, we are full of passion and life. Then, the clamp of societal norms kicks in to beat our creativity into submission. We become the victims of what society feels we need to think and act. Remember when you were young and your parents would say "stop day dreaming"? Ever here someone tell you to stop fooling around and get serious. Even though there is a time and place for everything, the art of mental creativity and desire visualization is the essence of all genius, invention and, ultimately, riches. Passion is the blueprint for how all dreams are formulated.

When asked what your passion is, it should not be to get rich. Riches are a result of spending your time and energy on your passion. If your passion is riches, you will be susceptible to many get rich schemes, any and all business ideas and even negative interactions in the quest for money. Your true and sustainable riches and profits are hidden in your passion.

Whether you know your passion or have yet to discover your passion, the following exercises are a great way to find, validate and solidify anyone's passion.

First, create two lists. The first one is 100 things you would like to do before you die. The other list is the top 25 things you love to do. The length of the lists is not important. What is important is the content of the list. Our minds think in pictures and creating a list, and writing it down, sparks the creativity needed to rediscover your true self interests and passions. From these lists, pull the top 10 most interesting or exciting to you (it should be 5 from each respective list). Then start having conversations with your friends and family about those 10 things. Challenge them to agree, disagree and debate on the top 10 things. You might be surprised on the perception others have on your passions. Also ask them to come up with their top 3 things they think you might be passionate about. Sometimes we over look what comes natural to us which can be our hidden genius.

Being human means we are dynamic, complex beings with multiple interests. Do not feel confined to finding that golden passion. Stuart Knight said, "*finding your passion is not about finding a needle in a haystack. It is about discovering the many needles in that haystack and trying to do as many of them as possible in this lifetime*". Remember, passions are the blueprint to dreams so start dreaming, jot them down and pick your passion.

While you develop your passion, be conscious of those around you with whom you share your dreams. Any and all accomplishments began with a thought. The problem is hundreds of thousands of people around the world never see the light at the end of the tunnel. All they see are the obstacles in front of them. Anyone who tells you something cannot be done is usually the same person who has not accomplished any of their passions. You will never meet a self made millionaire who did not acquire their riches with the absence of passion – It is that simple!

Be the change you seek

"Be the change you seek" is the famous quote by Barack Obama. Many people have a desire to do something but get started or start half heartedly. Jerry Rice said, "*Today I will do what others won't, so tomorrow I can accomplish what others can't.*" You have to get started if you want to accomplish anything. Indecision to get started NOW will become your decision to procrastinate and not get moving. This is a saying that my father would always tell me, "Things at rest tend to stay at rest". What he was telling me without being bossy was to not wait and do my homework first before I played video games. It is that same mentality the rich have that the majority of people do not take serious enough. You must do what you must today, so you can do what you want later. To start is the beginning and most important aspect of all journeys to riches.

Saying you must start is easy enough but procrastination can be a seductive distraction. Below are some fast suggestions to "make procrastination wait" as you go on your journey to riches

- Try not to choose low impacting tasks over high value activities – Try swinging for the fences with everything you do.
- Be aware that being busy is not the same as being productive –Try to do the most important things first every day.

- Perfection is a myth. Things do not always have to be perfect. Heck, the best baseball players hit no more than 35% of the times at bat.
- Know that insecurity comes from not knowing the steps. Plan and write down all the tasks you want to accomplish.
- Know that success is not about being the smartest but those who have the least amount of excuses and ready to take action.

Once you start taking action you must shift gears and get revved up about your passion. You must start to indulge yourself in the activities and things that excite you the most. This does not mean going out wasting your resources to get it but it could be mean educating yourself on it, visualizing yourself in possession of it, or simply learning about people who are involved in it. Sounds simple but many people wait for the perfect situation, perfect offer, or the perfect sign from God to get started. In order to become rich, you must be consumed with your passion. It must be on your mind the majority of your day. Below are some easy to follow rules in keeping that motor going as you take your passion and embed it in your mind body and soul into your journey to becoming rich.

First, you must believe in your passion.

You must champion the things you care most about, if the things you care most about are to be attracted to you. If someone asks you what you are passionate about, if you are not excited to tell someone/anyone about what drives you, it will be very difficult to drive you close to realizing it. Who would have thought that creating a website that limited your character limit to a mere 124 characters and telling the world what you are doing would be a successful business venture?

Well, the makers of Twitter had a passion for the concept; in 2011, it was one of the most profitable companies and helped reshape marketing efforts around the world. If you want to be rich, be proud of what you are passionate about.

I spoke about this earlier but I cannot stress enough the importance of starting where you stand and not looking at what you lack. The more you give attention to the things that are not in your possession, the more you will give power to that lack.

Focusing on lack is not the foundation of any rich person. They focus on how to get what they want, not what they don't have. In all situations, be thankful and appreciative for what you have and get excited about the potential to acquire all you desire in life.

As you start working on your passion, be consciously aware of your surroundings. Be open to the endless opportunities around you. Take advantage of and approach every opportunity that presents itself with confidence and vigour. I am not saying to pursue every opportunity but always be ready to hear ideas, concepts and plans to help you achieve your plan to riches. This openness to see the vast resources in your current surroundings will yield great results if you infuse a positive attitude, and move fast with action to move forward or move on.

As you move forward or move on, whatever your decision – Stay positive. When you are positive, it creates the positive atmosphere you live in. I was listening to Bob Proctor in an episode of *6 minutes to Success* which talked about creating a positive atmosphere. Atmosphere doesn't just happen; it takes the human mind to create it. Robert C. Hinds who is one of the top commenters provided some great additions to this concept. He stated, "*Creating a great, positive, atmosphere is something that we can all do. It is our choice. Creating great atmosphere is all about Energy. It is about you, your posture, your smile, your outlook, your attitude. When you are in a 'great atmosphere', you will become aware of how good you feel. It will surround you and flow to you and through you and then guess what...you look around and you are surrounded by people who have great attitudes too, who also create great atmospheres. Being in great surroundings will help you to express your greatness and your creativity. You will start to harmonize with the people around you, attracting to yourself the desires that dominate your thoughts. Whether it is in a mastermind group or a great network marketing organization, being around great people and a great atmosphere is essential and conducive to growth. Don't hold back and don't let other people keep you small. You have a giant inside of you, ready to step out. You just need to open the door for the giant step out".* When I read this, it made me think of my own personal story on the power of positive thinking and the importance to think positive about every situation.

What I am about to share is the moment that I truly understood the power of positive thinking and provided me with evidence that situations don't always change but people can.

Personal reflections: One day I decided to visit my mother and instead of driving, I decided to walk since she only lived about 20 minutes away. Now, usually I called before I would visit her but on that day, I wanted to surprise her. As I started on my journey, I realized I forgot her house keys on my kitchen counter. It was not a big issue at the time because it was Saturday and she usually does her laundry so she could always open the door for me. As I turned on her street, I noticed a dog a few houses away from my mother's house. Depending on the size of the dog, I get a bit nervous around them. Seeing the dog, I instantly started looking for my exit strategy if the dog should attack. As I got closer, sure enough the dog saw me and raced toward me barking as if to say "lunch is being served". I ran as fast as I could and jumped on the hood of a minivan. I was too high on the van to be bitten but what lasted for minutes, seemed like hours. I was yelling for help and for someone to come get this dog away from me. Finally, the owner came and apologized as the dog had escaped from the back yard. As I got off the van trembling slightly, I started having an internal conversation. I knew that everything happens for a reason and I should remain positive, but what was positive about what happened? As I racked my brain for answers, I approached my mother's front door and started knocking. As I continued knocking for a bit, I started getting a feeling in my gut that my efforts were in vain. If only I remembered to bring her keys, I would not be standing outside knocking like an idiot. It was apparent that my mother was not home and I should have called before I came over. In a state of defeat, I asked God, what could possibly be the positive side to wasting 20 minutes of my day to be attacked by a dog and find out my mother was not home? Now, I have to waste another 20 minutes to walk back home. I pause the story here because sometimes when you speak to God, you get an answer. I heard someone say we as humans never fail any of God's tests, we just keeping talking them until we pass them. I used to wonder why things happened, but then as I developed my prosperity mindset, I started to uncover the positive side to more situations. It was what happened next that solidified my belief that in everything, one should remain positive. As I began my walk back home, I noticed a young mother pushing a baby carriage across the street. Then, I noticed an elderly lady cross my path – THAT'S WHEN IT HIT ME. If I did not visit my mother, and got attacked by that dog, that young mother, her baby or the elderly lady would have been attacked. I know they would not have had the ability to jump on the hood of the minivan the way that I did. I would rather have a few seconds of terror and avert what could have been a much worse and tragic situation. I also learned that if I did not forget to bring my mother's keys, I would have never had the pleasure of seeing firsthand the reason why things happen and the importance of positive thinking.

Even though staying positive in all situations is important, what is more important is to think positive in your abilities and keep a strong, healthy self-image. Poor self image is the cancer of all people who do not reach the levels of riches they deserve. People can have a positive outlook on life and situations but if they do not have the power of self, and believe in their God given abilities, they will fail. Confidence attracts riches every time.

The story of the "get rich" Guru

There is a parable about a man who wanted to be rich and successful that encapsulates what real passion is all about. The best version I heard of this parable is the one illustrated by Eric Thomas. Now, I altered the story for the purposes of this book but the meaning behind it remains powerful and true.

As the story starts, there is a young man who was blessed enough to find a Success Guru. He mustered up enough courage to ask him what the secret to becoming rich and successful was. The young man told the Guru, "I am a young man with a passion for music but I am not where I want to be in life". The Guru looked deep into the man's eyes and said to meet him on the beach at the crack of dawn the next day if he really wants to become rich and successful. The young asked why at the beach and why at the crack of dawn? The Guru started to walk away and just repeated what he had just instructed, "If you want to become rich and successful, meet me on the beach at the crack of dawn".

The next morning, the young man put on his best suit, and headed out the beach. When he arrived at the crack of dawn like the Guru instructed, he noticed not a soul was there - Did the Guru forget? Did the Guru change his mind? After a few moments of pondering what to do next, the young man saw the Guru off in the distance by the shore. The Guru then motioned for him to join him by the sea shore. As the young man approached, sand started getting in his dress shoes. He started to feel funny about whether he should have worn a suit to the beach. When he reached the Guru, he said, "Morning, sir. Can you now tell me the secret to becoming rich and successful?" The guru kept a straight face and said if you want to become rich and successful, follow me.

Then, he started to walk out in the sea. The young man looked the Guru for a minute then came to the resolution this must be a test so he followed. As the young man got close, the Guru said, "If you want to become rich and successful, follow me". Then, the Guru moved out in the sea a little more. The young man said, "I cannot swim". The Guru was not deterred in his actions, he raised his voice and stated, "If you want to become rich and successful, follow me". Every time the young man got close, the Guru would move further and say, "If you want to become rich and famous follow me". Then, once the water reached the young man's shoulders the guru put his hands on the young man's head in a fatherly position and said lovingly, "Are you ready to become rich and successful?"

Eager to learn the secrets, the young man smiled and said, "Yes". In that moment, the Guru took the young man's head and submerged it in the sea. The young man started struggling to pull himself out of the water but the Guru was too strong. The young man started fighting to pull his head up to no avail, then just before he was about to drawn, the Guru pulled him up. As the young man struggled for air, he coughed and yelled, "Why did you do that?" The Guru looked in his eyes, similar to when they first met, and said gently, "When you were under water, what were you thinking about?" Still coughing and gasping for air, he said, "I just wanted to breathe!"

Now, the face of the Guru turned stern and he confirmed, "If you want to be rich and successful with your passion, you must want it as bad as you want to breathe". You must want it more than anything else in the world. Breathing is the essence of life and until you treat your passions in the same manner, you will never become rich and successful.

Eric Thomas went on to say after the parable that the problem with many individuals today is they want to become rich but many do not want it bad enough. People tend to race home to watch their favourite TV show or line up for hours, even days, to get the latest electronic gadget that is on sale. However, when it comes to their passion and pursuing it, they attack it half-heartedly. If you really want to become rich, you have to take your passion and make it priority number 1 in your life. You have to cut down on your "play" time and get going on developing your passion. If you want to be rich and successful, you must be willing to sacrifice who you are today in order to become what you want to be tomorrow.

MOVE FROM WORK STYLE TO LIFE STYLE

"Nothing can add more power to your life than concentrating all your energies on a limited set of targets"

– Nido Qubein

The Power of Motivation

Personal reflections: As stated earlier, one of my main passions is helping others reach their full potential. A trip to my parents' place of birth in the beautiful St. Vincent and the Grenadines helped show the power of motivation. The island is extremely small with a population of about 120,000 people, yet I have never seen such motivation to have a "North American" style of life. My uncle Tracey is by no means a man of great monetary wealth but his motivation to provide for his family is a testament to what can be accomplished when you are motivated. My cousins want for nothing and have been provided all the opportunities necessary to excel in life. Watching my uncle provide for his family is a direct reflection of the amazing accomplishments any person can do if they have the power of motivation to fuel their daily efforts.

The easiest way to fuel your daily efforts is via indentifying your passion – it will naturally motivate your efforts.

The transitioning of your life from mediocrity to riches starts from transitioning your actions. Transitioning your work style into a lifestyle is being able to embed your passion into everything you do. You must recognize that you have to change what you are currently doing. It is just as the saying goes, "To have what you never had, you must do what you never did". Everyone on earth is provided the same 24 hours in a day. The average person spends the majority of their day at work or doing things related to their 9-5 job. So, unless, you are already in your dream job, why do you put yourself through such bondage? The answer is money. It is really a paradox. People hate to work at their job but take the pay check encouraging more work. Now, I am not suggesting your quit your job but I am saying to take your passion and start planning your exit strategy from the Rat Race. When you transition from work style and integrate your efforts into your personal life, it becomes your life style. If you are not spending your spare time fulfilling your passion, you are wasting your life's time and lying to your Soul.

Some people will say they do not have spare time to work on the things they love. That is the biggest lie a person can tell to themselves. If you take public transit to work, you can read and educate yourself on your passions. If you drive to work, you can listen to audio tapes that assist in your passions. Instead of watching TV, spend time on your passion and the things you love. If you have dependants like children or an elderly person, spend your time engaging them with your passion (you will be very surprised on how receptive they will be to it). It is YOUR time to get enthusiastic about your passion(s) and start taking action to change your work style to a life style.

Raymond Aaron spoke about motivation in one of his newsletters and, instead of paraphrasing, I am going to share it word for word because it is so powerful. He wrote, "…*Motivation wears off. It's like a shower. You cannot stay clean forever from one shower; you need to keep taking showers every day to stay clean. Similarly, you will need to keep pumping yourself up if you wish to stay motivated. It is an empty pursuit.*

Fortunately, I teach my mentored students that there is a goal far more rewarding than being motivated. That loftier goal is to do only what you love. When you do what you love, you are automatically and internally motivated.

Here's how you do that…

So, the wisdom is not to pretend you like a task you dislike by pumping yourself up with some motivational sayings or audios. Rather, the wisdom is to identify what you love and then focus your career, your income, your learning, your energy on that which you love. When you do, your income will rise sharply and you will never have to pump yourself up with motivation. You will be internally and permanently high.

Personally, I love riding my unicycle. I do not need to get motivated to ride my unicycle; I am wired motivated because I love it. I love teaching. I do not need to get motivated to teach; I come wired ready and eager to teach. I love writing bestselling books to inspire people. I love writing interesting articles. I need to motivational audios to force me to pretend that I like these activities; I really actually do love them.

So, do not seek to simply get motivated; rather, seek to do what you love. Record a goal each month to do more of what you love and less of what you do not love. When you put your creativity in that direction, you will arrive at fascinating answers that will change your life…"

Notice Raymond Aaron is talking about internal motivation, not a pep talk from a mentor or coach. Unless you have that internal spark, you might be motivated for a day, a week, even a month but sooner or later, you will fall back to your old ways. Even with that internal spark, you must cultivate and build it into a fire. Motivation is like an insecure child that needs constant re-enforcement, examples to model from and care. If people only required to listen to a powerful speech or started a solid list of how they want to become rich, everyone would already be rich but the reality there is so much more to motivation.

Motivation is more than writing down goals, listening to pep talks and planning for success.

Yes those are important factors but the human brain does not operate by words. We all think in pictures. I want you to NOT THINK ABOUT A TURTLE. I REPEAT DO NOT THINK ABOUT A TURTLE, NOT EVEN A SMALL TURTLE, A BIG TURTLE OR A FAT TURTLE – DO NOT THINK OF A TURTLE – TURTLE TURLTE TURTLE.

Now I ask you, did a picture of a turtle pop in your brain? A great speaker can motivate you with their words and you can get inspired by reading text. However, unless you take these external stimuli and convert them into mental pictures, motivation can only go so far. These stimuli can come via mental affirmations of your success in the present tense and powerful visualizations. You need to daydream about your riches and make them real. Take your passion, focus on them and really imagine what your riches look like and all the good you can provide society with your resources.

To be truly motivated, you must take your passion, focus on it so much that every thought, action and habit becomes a reflection of your desire to become rich.

The Power of focus

The way to take your passion and cultivate a rich lifestyle from it comes down to one thing – Focus. Focus is the engine that takes your passion down the river to riches. John Assaraf gave a powerful visual on how visuals work. Take the concept of light. The sun's rays can warm your face on a summer afternoon and with a little focus, you can be susceptible to sunburn. Take the same light from the sun's Rays and use the focus of a magnifying glass, you can start a fire. Taking it one step further, with extreme focus, light can be amplified to create a laser that can cut through rock.

If you are unable to focus in on what you want in life, you need to ask yourself why? What is preventing you from taking charge of your mind, body and soul? Usually, the level of a person's focus comes down to the level of motivation within them. Motivation is defined as the reason or reasons one has for acting or behaving in a particular way. It can also be defined as the general desire or willingness of someone to do something. If you want to become rich and your motivation is strong enough, extreme focus will allow you to realize your dreams.

Focus is super charged when mixed with constant motivation. Motivation either comes from the desire to gain or the fear of loss. The desire to gain is a result of knowing what your passion is and how to gain access to everything associated with it. Until you focus on your passion, motivation becomes ineffective and stagnant. Desire to gain is an internal mental conversation. Without focus, that internal conversation and energy are focused on other less important things.

On the other hand, the fear of loss comes from the response given from your environment. Simeon Ben Eleazar said, "*Greater is he who acts from love than he who acts from fear.*" The healthiest form of motivation is not in response to loss (such as a job, relationship or status), but from the proactive desire to expand on your current situation. Become happy and grateful for your current position in life because, with the right focus and motivation, the only way you can go is up and beyond to the land of riches

The Razor's Edge

Personal reflections: When I get a fresh hair cut and shave, I feel like a million bucks. Anytime I get ready for an important event or need to look my best, I make sure my head is lined up and my face is baby soft. The thing that drives me crazy is after about a day or two, the hair starts to grow back. Once it grows back, the transformation it creates is very interesting. Not only do I look different, I feel and act differently. For one, I look about 5 years older. Secondly, I do not feel comfortable wearing suits because I do not feel like a million bucks anymore.

The difference is only a millimetre, but that less than a millimetre of hair growth had the ability to change my entire self-perception as well as the perception others had of me. That fine line of difference is also the difference between someone taking me seriously as a businessman or just someone wearing a suit.

This is a great example of the power of the Razor's Edge concept. A fraction of additional effort can mean the difference between being part of the masses and standing out in the crowd. When you take your passion and integrate it into your everyday life, it will have profound results over time. Many people intend to start working on their passion; other people start working on theirs. It is that little bit of extra effort that gains momentous results. When I was in the corporate world, I decided to come into work 30 minutes earlier to focus on my passion. Those 30 minutes were spent educating myself, utilizing resources that supported it and engaging others who shared the same interest on the topic. After a year, the time spent would have been the equivalent of taking 5, 13-week 2 hour classes in school. The Razor's Edge concept not only works in transforming your work style into a life style, it helps to build new habits that align with the Rich. Waking up early, dressing for success, constantly reading, maintaining a healthy lifestyle are all small variables that, continued over time, will result in you becoming the cream of the crop.

Another example of the benefits of the Razor's Edge is in track and field. In 2009, at the Berlin Games, Usain Bolt won the world record for the 100 meter dash with a time of 9.58 seconds. With this astonishing time, he won the Gold Medal, millions of dollars in sponsorship deals, and become famous. The second place runner was 9.71 seconds which is only 13 hundredths of a second slower. That miniscule fraction difference is what created fortune and fame for Usain Bolt.

Now, I want to move from conceptual analysis to actual tactics.

In order to incorporate the Razor's edge in your life, here are the basics of what you should be doing:

Watch less Television: It is so easy to become wrapped in the drama and intrigue of a good TV show or movie. The story lines and plots can be extremely fascinating and addictive. There are two main problems with television; the first is the amount of time that seems to blow by when watching it. The second is that it is not YOU on the screen. Why spend countless hours watching the lives of others and not focusing on your own life?

I heard Bob Proctor say many people are like extras in their own movie. People have opinions, comments and are aware of so many aspects of the stars on TV and little to no opinion on what they want out of their own lives. BE the star of your own movie. Invest more time and effort away from the "Boob Tube" and spend just a little more time on your passion. It can be as little as 30 minutes a day to start. As you get more and more into your passion, you will notice the 30 minutes become an hour, then two and so on. Less television equals more time to focus on your passion

Wake up earlier: Waking up earlier provides more time for you to get your day started and allows you to not rush so much in doing it. It also allows you the time to prepare your day and meditate on the important tasks that must be accomplished. Waking up earlier is not always the easiest task but the more you plan before you go to bed, the easier it becomes.

Try making breakfast and laying out your clothes the night before. It will free up some more morning time. Also, set two alarm clocks one by your bed and the other across the room (forcing you to get up and turn it off). Lastly, try praying or meditating before going to bed on your dreams. It will help lower the stresses of the day and get you in a better state of mind to have a sound sleep so you are not as tired when you wake up

Manage your Time: Once you wake up early, you need to start your day with a plan. Time management is the key to all success. Every second of your day is a gift from God. A gift that once provided is gone forever.

a. Do most important things first
b. Map out your day
c. Take breaks to recharge and de-clutter your mind from negative thoughts and inhibitions

Once you have a schedule for your day and you stick to it, over time, you will notice more time appearing to refocus on the most important things. Your multitasking and productivity capabilities will also increase.

Read more books: Reading is basically mind exercises. Everyone knows exercise is good for the body. Well, reading is healthy for the mind and soul. Instead of being reactive and deciphering information that comes to you, be proactive and control that information. Learn more about topics that inspire and shape your understanding of your passion.

The easiest way to become a subject matter expert on any topic is to read about it. Educate yourself so you can use the knowledge to bridge creativity and logic. Borrow books from the library (it's free!) or start reading downloadable books for when you are by your computer or on your phone. Your mind and soul crave exercise just like you body so start flexing those brain muscles.

Live healthier: While you flex those brain muscles, do not forget the machine – your body. Make a conscious effort to take in less fatty foods that make you feel sluggish and tired. Look for foods with energy like fruits, greens and LOTS of water. I am not a nutritionist but I have found that Chris Guerriero's (Chris@EnergyFactor.TV) program was easy to follow and worked as it related to energizing my body and putting me in the right direction for a healthier lifestyle. Now take, all this added energy and use it as fuel. Exercise more. Park your car further from all destinations on purpose and have a brisk walk. Take the stairs instead of the elevator. These little things will help you start on the road to a healthier lifestyle

Dress for success: This is an overlooked variable. When people first meet you, they judge you by your appearance. Yes, it is true you cannot judge a book by its cover but in order to read the pages of the book therein, the cover is what attracts people to read the book. Do not dress for how you feel, dress for how you want to feel and how you want to be perceived. I am not saying go out and waste money on clothes. I am saying, when you leave your home, dress for success. Overdressing is never a bad thing and people are attracted to a well put together individual. If you look like a million bucks, you will begin to act like you have a million bucks. Next thing you know, you have a million bucks. Take pride in your attire!

Go the extra mile: This factor encompasses everything in the book - In everything you do, go the extra mile. Provide that little extra effort to receive amazing results. Be it at your job or at play, give it your all, and then give a little more. It does not have to be much but give something. Going the extra mile can be for your own efforts and it can be to help others. There is magic in creating the "wow" factor for those around you and yourself.

Taking your passion and integrating it into your everyday life is the first step to riches. If your passion is in line with your current work of business, then this chapter should be a time to reflect and refine your efforts. If your passion is not aligned with your current job or business, this is not a ploy to quit and start anew. What you should be doing is find ways to incorporate it into your job wherever possible and find ways to pursue your passion when you are not working. Create a hobby with your passion and start small. Eventually, as your passion builds momentum, you can start making a new career out of what you love.

STEP 2
MAP OUT YOUR GOALS

"Our goals can only be reached through a vehicle of a plan, in which we must fervently believe, and upon which we must vigorously act. There is no other route to success."

Stephen A. Brennan

GIVE YOUR GOALS LIFE

"God gives every bird a worm,
but he does not throw it into the nest."

Swedish Proverb

Marketing 101

Believe it or not, like it or not, everything is Marketing. Everything! From someone working in sales to a baby crying for attention; it is all about doing what is required for desired results. The paradox of marketing is that the basic concept of marketing is so easy to understand yet the majority of people do not utilize it. People may use parts of marketing concepts but when planning out a plan for success (in any endeavor), all of what I call the 5 points of stardom is important to ensure a successful endeavor. These points are Product, Position, Price, Promotion, and Place (the 5 Ps).

From this point, you should aim to integrate as many of the 5 points of stardom in everything you do. I will only provide a brief understanding of these 5 points so you have a clearer idea of each and how you can utilize in every aspect of your life and not only for your path to riches. I do encourage you to learn more about marketing and branding as it will shape the way you look at all of your surroundings. From the people you engage, to how present your product or service to the marketplace to the way you carry yourself in public. Marketing and branding are like air. They are everywhere and without them, you will perish.

Point of Position: This is where you have to summon your creative faculties and state what makes you special. There is nothing new under the sun just variations of timeless topics. Your position is what makes you different from the person next to you. If you are into real estate investing and you have a knack for finding over valued properties, then your positioning in the market should be "the one who finds undervalued homes with ease". Positioning also controls all the other aspects of the marketing Ps. It is what governs the perception of your offering. How do people view what you bring? If you are perceived as low value, you may need to tweak your position in the market. If you are perceived as best in market for customer service, then that becomes your position and it can allow you to be flexible with the other marketing Ps (such as set a higher price for the perceived value).

Point of Product: In traditional marketing, the product is whatever you give the customer. It can be a physical product or it can be an intangible service. Take this understanding and convert to your path to riches and you will understand that your passion can easily become a product or service. If your passion is to create a product for sale, a service to offer, or concept to champion, the first point to stardom is to understand what it is.

In the last chapter, we learned how to discover your passion(s) and now it is time to itemize all the products and services you can create from it. If your passion is food, your product can be your expertise on all the ingredients and quantities which make a certain dish taste amazing. Then, you can convert your expertise into a cook book or sell it to a chef for profit. Your product is whatever you make it

Point of Price: The price set takes into account the cost to produce/make the product or service you are offering and leaves a buffer to allow for profits. Depending on the value you are bringing to the market, you should set your price accordingly. The easiest way to enter any market is to have the price as low as possible to build your customer/client base. However, low entry point can also be perceived as low value in the market. You should always aim to underoffer and overcommit. Whatever price you set should be less than the perceived value of the offering. As long as you are able to maintain good margins on your costs, you should always aim to overdeliver on the price you set.

Point of Place: After you have convinced a potential purchaser of your goods and services, and that they need to do business with you, you have to provide a way to collect money. In a new economy, the power of global shipping and e-commerce allows for increased places a potential customer can spend dollars with you. When considering where someone can purchase what you have to offer, you want to ensure it can be delivered in a timely manner and with good post sale service. The best type of customer is a repeat one and statistics show it take about 6 times as much effort to attract a new customer than it does to maintain an existing one. Your after sale efforts is, therefore, even more important than the sale itself. You must dedicate a good chunk of your time ensuring you are providing exceptional value to your existing base (word of mouth marketing is the best free tool at your disposal).

Point of Promotion: This is probably the most important point as is brings aspects of all the other points together. It allows the world access to what you offer. It also educates them on why they should do business with you. There are many subsections within promotion, from advertising and publicity to social media and branding. For the purposes of ensuring your passions line up with your plan to riches, Branding should be your focal point. Branding is a combination of how you want to be viewed in pubic and how the public actually views you. For instance, when you go on a plane, you have 1st class and you have economy. One allows you to board first, sit in more comfortable seats and you get a little extra care. The other is more for the masses where the price is cheaper but you get less customer service attention. Both customers take the same plane to the same destination but the 1st class experience is branded as a better flying experience.

However you intend to brand yourself, all your marketing efforts, the way you conduct yourself and treat others must be a reflection of your brand. If you look to be the real estate investor who finds gems, you better have the inside track to deals. If you want to be perceived as having amazing customer service, you better be prepared to go the extra mile for every potential customer. In order make your brand believable, you must walk the walk and talk the talk. Your branding success will be measured by your interaction feedback, niche market acceptance and network growth. If you want to learn more about the power of branding, go to www.howtobrandyourproduct.com for details

Where did the Dreamer go?

Becoming rich is in your grasp once you take your passion and formulate a plan to better integrate it into your life.

Some people say such a comment is easier said than done. Some people say that in order to make money, you need to first have money. While having money makes it easier to make money, there is no direct correlation to such a claim. Real money is made through creative thought which is auctioned by a definite plan to see it to fruition. If the idea is sound, investors and support systems can always be created to help finance the effort. Some people also say you need an education to become rich. Although an education helps to build a solid foundation for understanding concepts and processes to create and keep wealth, it still comes down to your mind and knowing that your end goal is to become rich. Richard Branson, Bill Gates and 50 Cent are just a few examples of people who used their creative faculties as the source of their respective empires.

Lastly, I often hear people say they want to wait until the economy improves before real money can be made. This is the most outrageous statement of all. I think the masses have tricked themselves into believing this. The fact is that there are more millionaires created in bad economic times than in good ones. Reason is when most people are panicking about, worrying about and hoarding their current resources, those who use their creative mind are thinking of ways to capitalize on them. Creativity is the key to taking your passion and putting a twist on it that stimulates a plan to make it a reality. This is the Millionaire Mindset. In order to become rich, you must take your dream and turn it into a plan. A goal is really only a dream with a plan. You give your dreams life when you plan them out.

To witness creativity in its purest form, I recommend spending time with children. They have the ability to dream big and believe they can do anything. Ask almost any child what they want to be when they grow up and their answers are always exciting. From an astronaut, sports superstar to famous singer; children tend to dream big and believe it can happen for them. Then, society comes along and continuously attempts to crush their dreams via family, friends and media. Instead of inspiring all dreams, people consciously and subconsciously sabotage them. When I was a child, I wanted to become a basketball superstar. At the time, I was the best in my class and, eventually I was the best in grade school. I thought I would have the opportunity to play against the basketball greats and I would even have my out sports card. Then, the limiting beliefs of others started to trickle down into my mind and impacted those dreams. First, I stopped growing and people started saying things like, "If only you were taller", then came the statistics that less than 1% of people who want to become a sports star make it to the top. Lastly, there were the folks who said you are talented but you are not good enough to make it at a professional level. Luckily I was a creative child and had many dreams and aspirations so I think I still did very well for myself in the end as it relates to being successful in life.

However, what if I did not have those negative opinions bombarding me? What if I did not listen to any of them and focused on my dream? What if I took my dream and formulated a plan to see it to fruition? Les Brown said "Aim for the Sun, because even if you miss, you will be amongst the stars". What should have happened was for me to acknowledge my challenges but still press on with my dreams with a plan to see them through. I am only 5'8 but so was Spud Webb (and he won a slam dunk contest against a man who was 6'8). Another example was Mugsie Bogues. He was only 5'1 and he had an amazing NBA career. Even if I did not make it to the NBA, who is to say what would have come from it. I could have played in Europe or been a basketball coach in the NBA. Who knows what could have been. Each and every one of us must become a master of the external influences that enter our brain and reject any notion that is contrary to the fulfillment of our passion and dreams.

Based on how children dream and hope for wonder and excitement in their adult life, I ask you to take some time of self reflection and try to remember when you were a child. Think about what you wanted to be when you grew up. What did you want to accomplish in your adult years? Now, fast forward to the present – are you doing what you dreamt about? Chances are that you are not doing it (why else would you be reading this book?). The sad thing is people tend to fall into the trap of being comfortable and settling for what life brings them. There is so much more to life than what you have been given. Now is the time to tap into those creative faculties that have been dormant since you were a child. Once you learn to tap into your creative mind, you will be amazed at the power and diversity of what your mind can conjure up just by thinking about your passion.

Transform Dreams to Goals

I heard someone say, "Start anywhere because anywhere is a place and it will lead you everywhere". This statement is really what everyone should be doing. Your passion and dreams are useless until you put them into action. Action puts flesh to faith, so get started now. Many people wait on that perfect sign from God or the perfect opportunity to show them the path. The best time to begin something was yesterday, the second best time is right now.

Create your goal and start it anywhere, anyhow, now. It does not matter how small your initial efforts are, still start. Many a tidal wave started from a drop of water in the ocean. The domino effect from the actions you take in setting your goals will change your life and help you capture the riches you deserve. Take your dreams and turn them into goals – Now!

Transforming your dreams to goals involved four basic tasks. Those four steps are:

- creating the goal in your mind,
- writing it down,
- making it specific and measurable for your evaluation, and
- making yourself accountable to seeing it through.

This is where many people fail to take their dreams and convert them into riches. Your goals do not have to be an elaborate formula where you have to gain access to different resource tools and monitoring systems. As my University, professors used to always tell me – Just K.I.S.S: **K**eep **I**t **S**imple **S**tupid. By no means am I calling you stupid, but I am saying to not complicate things with over planning and thought. So let us dive into these three basic steps:

Step 1 – Break down your passion: If you do not have your passion(s) formulated, I urge you to stop reading, go back and find your passion first. If you have already decided on your vehicle to get you to your riches, then you must take the time to analyze it now. What area of your passion should you focus on? Will you create a complementary product or service for your passion? Will you teach others how to enjoy your passion as well? These are just some of the questions you should ask yourself.

For example, let us use the passion for cars to illustrate the breaking down process. Sam has a passion for cars. He does not have the technical knowledge to manufacture or repair cars; heck, he does not even know how to change a flat tire. Despite this, cars are still his passion. He loves the look, sound and smell of any sports car on the road. Sam is, however, a good writer. As a child, he would write short stories, poems and plays. Sam could create his empire by starting a magazine dedicated to cars. He could interview experts in the field, review the latest cars and even promote and sell various car accessories. Now, someone might say, "there are many magazines that do just that, why should he enter a saturated market?"

That is where further research and creativity are required. Sam should use the incompetence of the average reader angle to gain his competitive advantage. Not being able to understand all the technical jargon could be his unique selling proposition. He could create a magazine for people like him – those who love sports cars but do not know much about them. Sam could use simple language and terms that anyone could understand and enjoy. Sam's goal could be to create a sports car magazine that caters to the average guy who loves sports cars but does not understand all the technical aspects to it. Sam could have segments interviewing experts and have them explain the car in basic terms. Sam could have segments on tips everyday people could use to help make their car perform better. If Sam focuses on what makes his experience, he will be surprised at the number of other people who feel the same way and would not mind paying for his magazine.

To capitalize on your passion does not mean you have to be an expert in all respects. Try jotting down everything you can think of as it relates to your passion. What is missing that you would like to see? What could be improved? Are there complementary services you can provide? Is this a brand new idea? What about the negative aspects of your passion, is there an opportunity to capitalize on it? Can you help change the perception? Is there a market for the negative aspect?

Step 2 – Write down your goal: Studies have shown that if you do not write down the things you would like to accomplish, the probability of them not being completed is high. All successful companies write down their business and marketing plans to help focus their efforts and help commit mind, body and soul to the task. Since we are all a company of one, it only makes sense to also put our goals to paper. Taking our goals and committing them to paper reminds our brain there is work to do in attaining it. It is also the starting place if any planning and action steps are to be taken. I heard a man say "goals to paper is the skeleton for which the meat of all successes wraps itself around". Simply put, you need to write down your goals if you want to really digest what you want in life.

It is important to remember to use action-oriented words when putting together your goals. For example, it is not enough to have a goal to become rich as such a goal as that is too vague. A good example would be, "I will raise $100,000 to fund my real estate investments this year". Writing down your goals is the beginning of your business plan and your business plan is the beginning of your path to riches. There is a myth that it takes a lot of money to create a business plan or creating a business plan is too complex for the average person. The reality is creating a business plan is easy and solidifies your path. Go online and look for business plan templates to get you started on writing it all down. Many of these online business templates are free. They also systemize writing your thoughts, dreams and passions to put you in a place to secure investors and like-minded joint partners. A business is a crucial platform to organize your thoughts and revise aspects of how you will achieve your riches

Step 3 – Make your goal specific and measurable: This step is a follow up to writing down your goal. In order to ensure you achieve your goal, you have to make it specific and measurable. The reason is that you need an indicator that lets you know you are approaching success or have reached your destination for your goal. For example, people say I want to be happy. OK, so if you told me you were lonely, poor and sad and I told you a joke and you laughed, are you happy now? You may have had a moment of happiness but, overall, you would still not be happy. Another example is a marathon runner. It is not enough to desire to run until you cannot run anymore; they have a starting point and a specific finishing point. The time it takes to complete the race is the measurement. The finishing point (or goal) assists the runner in pushing themselves because they know they have not completed their specific goal – so they press on to the finish.

It is paramount to make your goal as specific as possible.

Too much information and detail are never a bad thing. You have to have the confidence and conviction to state exactly what the result is you want to achieve and you must define a clear timeline to get there. I quoted Les Brown earlier but I want to quote him again to aim for the moon because even if you miss, you will be among the stars. Making your goal specific and measurable can open doors you never imagined; doors that may not be part of the original plan. The process of making your goal specific and measurable will help to train and condition your brain to take action, better react to opportunities, and attempt to complete your goal.

Step 4 – Be accountable to your Goals: This step is a tricky yet important motivating tool in becoming rich. Later on, we will talk about being accountable via a mastermind but for now let us discuss the basics of the importance of being accountable to your goals. You have to share your goals with someone you trust. I am not suggesting you provide every detail but you should have a personal coach to assist in your vision and goal. All sports superstars have a coach and are accountable to them. These coaches motivate them, challenge them and assist in helping them reach their goal. The coach may not be as talented or skilled, but their input keeps the star on track and motivated. Do the same with your goal. You need that external input and feedback if you are to become rich. What makes this step tricky is finding the right person. You do not want to share your goal with someone who will turn around and steal it. You also want to ensure your coach has your (not their) best interest at heart, and at the same time champions your goal and helps you achieve them. Everyone needs to be accountable or the result is anarchy.

Many people make the error of setting an ultimate goal while creating many mini goals to get to the ultimate goal. Competitors in Strong Men competitions can pull airplanes with only a rope. They do this by pulling the rope with all their might and at first the plane goes nowhere, then little by little the plan starts to move. As they continue to pull the plane, they achieve many mini victories as the plane progresses forward to their end target. It is the same with goal setting start moving forward with mini goals as you progress to your end ultimate goal. I challenge you to set smaller, incremental goals for yourself and as you progress forward in your efforts, you will start to gain momentum. As your momentum increases, you have the option to adjust, improve and magnify your ultimate goal. Most importantly, don't forget to celebrate EVERY goal you accomplish. Reward yourself for your efforts no matter how big or small.

Setting goals is an important part of any business plan but setting a goal is only part of the picture. Implementing and taking steps to achieving them are even more important. Taking the steps for implementation is the beginning and taking action is the magical process to make things happen. Taking action is most important of all! Proverbs 14:23 says, "All hard work leads to riches but mere talk leads to poverty". All accomplishments and successes had a starting point. No matter the obstacles and challenges you will face, you must first start. In order to become, rich you must talk your thoughts and talking points and convert it into action. James Bryant Conant said, "Behold the Turtle, he only makes progress when he sticks his head out". You must first trust your passion and stick your head out of your current existence into the realm of what should be and get started. Learn how to identify which goals are important enough to commit to, and systematically work towards them by breaking them down into steps, establishing time lines, identifying resources needed, and benchmarking for success. Then, engage a trusted inner circle of confidants to be accountable to. Their input, care and motivation will help keep you on track

THE POWER OF PERSISTENCE

"Action puts flesh to faith"

Myles Munroe

Your efforts must persist

"Discipline is the bridge between goals & accomplishments"

- J.R.

The power of persistence is a force only experienced by those who dare to never give up. The Wright brothers made it possible to fly via the airplane via the power of persistence. They did not accomplish it on the first, second, third or thirtieth attempt. It was persistence that fuelled their success. Every inventor intuitively knows there are thousands of ways to not create their idea but only a few ways to create it. The only way to discover the successful method of their desire is through persistence.

Persistence is another main ingredient in the recipe to riches. It is the knowing that current results are not a reflection of future realities. Persistence is made easier from mastering daily success visualization and continuous affirmation activities. Being the architect of your blueprint to riches is all about trial and error, small successes and failures and understanding that all the errors and failures are what provide validity to your path to riches.

The topic of persistence as it relates to riches also includes understanding how to practice everything involved in turning our passion into profits. This includes practicing habits of the rich, practicing speaking intelligently about your goals and passions, and practicing continuous education in improving your understanding of your passion and desired results. Practice actually does create perfection. All close basketball games come down to which team can make more free throws. Michael Jordan, who is arguably the best player to ever live, had a free throw career average of 83.5% and he attributed his success rate in basketball to practice. Anyone who plays basketball will agree that practicing free throws is one of the most boring things to practice but in a game where every point counts, those behind–the-scene efforts are celebrated. Practice allows you to become the authority of your passion. Desiderius Erasmus said, "In the land of the blind the one eyed man is king". Practicing puts you in a place of expertise as your knowledge will be more than the person next to you. You do not have to be the best at your craft but practicing habits of the rich, practicing to master your craft and mastering yourself are required if you want to become rich.

Even with practice, persistence, and perseverance come the acknowledgement that you must never lose sight of your end goal of becoming rich. Once you improve your ability to keep on keeping on, it becomes easier to get caught in the process. In my early stages of personal development, I knew that educating myself was important and I was dedicated to taking 1 hour a day to that effort. The problem was I lost focus and was soaking up so much information without implementing them. Many an opportunity was missed because I got caught in the process. To better illustrate this, here is a story I read from an email received from my friend Nick Grimshawe. In the email, he shared a story called The Touchstone. It is a great example of the importance of persistence and how to not forget your end goal.

You must be dedicated and persistent in your efforts to do what is required to become rich. One pitfall you need to take heed about is to never lose sight of your end goal while you on your journey. It may be easy to get caught in the processes and rules to riches, but focusing on tactics while forsaking your strategic end goal can cause you to actually lose your way. This is a story of the "Touchstone" which illustrates this:

As the story goes, a poor man took the little money he had and purchased a special book. This special book contained the instructions to unlimited wealth. The book provided the approximate location of the "touchstone" which was a small pebble that could turn any common metal into pure solid gold. The difficult part was the touchstone lay among thousands and thousands of other small pebbles all of which looked identical. The only way to identify the touchstone was the warm feel in your hand while the other ordinary pebbles felt cold. Wanting to become rich, the poor man sold his few belongings and purchased some simple supplies for his journey. When he reached the location outlined in book, he could see that all the pebbles looked the same. His fear was that since all but one pebble was cold, he could spend a lifetime picking up the same cold pebbles again and again. Being a thinking man, he thought if he took any cold pebble he felt and threw it in the sea, he would avoid picking up the same pebble.

So it began. Day in and day out, the poor man would pick up cold pebbles and throw them in the sea. Without fail, he would grab a pebble, feel its coldness, and then throw it in the sea. This went on for days which turned into weeks which turned into months. However, one day, the poor man picked up a pebble and it was warm (it was the touchstone) but before he could compute he had a warm pebble in his hand, he threw it in the sea. The poor man had created a strong habit throwing pebbles into the sea that when the one pebble he should have saved presented itself, he still threw it away.

The same thing applies to recognizing your passion and watching out for signs to take things to the next level. To become rich, you do need focus, persistence and perseverance but never lose sight of your end goal. Opportunities are all around us and if we are not vigilant, and not recognize them, it is easy to have opportunities in your hand and in the same moment, throw it away.

"High achievers spot rich opportunities swiftly, make big decisions quickly and move into action immediately. Follow these principles and you can make your dreams come true."

Robert H. Schuller, Religious Minister

Transform Goals to Reality

"I would visualize things coming to me. It would just make me feel better. Visualization works if you work hard. That's the thing. You can't just visualize and go eat a sandwich."

Jim Carrey

Transforming goals to reality happens before your goals are materialized into their physical equivalent. To become truly rich, you have to be the master of your visualization, affirmation and meditative efforts. These activities are the internal motivation and neural conditioning mechanisms to riches. Daily visualization and continuous affirmations do two things: they rewire and solidify neurons in your brain to continue to manifest the desired outcome you seek. Just as any athlete needs to practise and condition their body, so does your brain need constant mental training that riches are in your grasp. To help increase the rate of effectiveness, you must include all your faculties. Beside visual, you must include hear, smell, taste and touch wherever possible. Whatever you think about most often expands in your life, and including all your faculties (such as taste, sight, smell, feel and hear) increases the speed of this expansion. So if you are constantly worried about not having enough money, you will get more life experiences of not having enough money. Focusing on opportunities to make money will get you a thousand times further than worrying about the lack of it.

But Power Visualization is more than just positive thinking. It's about putting your mind and body in the ideal place first, and then flooding your subconscious with a colourful experienced of life as you want it. The more relaxed you are, the more open your subconscious is to receive the messages you want to send it such as becoming rich. The more senses that you involve in your Power Visualization, the more of an impact it will have.

For example, let's say that you wanted to buy a new car. Just saying you want a "new car" is too vague a term. What kind of new car do you want? What colour is it and how will you feel when you are driving it? Notice I said when you are driving it – You have to believe it to see it. You need to be absolutely specific and detailed as possible. So to refine it, you may actually want a brand new, black 2012 BMW 6 Series with Red leather interior and 19 inch rims. You have to bring your desires to life if you want it.

Why is persistence, visualization, and detailing your desires so important? The simple answer is that is how your brain operates. That is how you will create the future you desire, by taking your passion, having your end goal in mind and continuing without interruption with your plan for success. Repetition is also required in changing paradigms or, better put, creating the habits you should have to create the mindset of the successful.

HOW THE BRAIN WORKS

Before we talk about how the brain works, I wanted to share a little brain game emailed to me from a friend I am not sure the source but when I read it, I was shocked to see my brain in action before my eyed. This is weird, but interesting if you can read it!

"7H15 M3554G3
53RV35 7O PR0V3
H0W 0UR M1ND5 C4N
D0 4M4Z1NG 7H1NG5!
1MPR3551V3 7H1NG5!
1N 7H3 B3G1NN1NG
17 WA5 H4RD BU7
N0W, 0N 7H15 LIN3
Y0UR M1ND 1S
R34D1NG 17
4U70M471C4LLY
W17H 0U7 3V3N
7H1NK1NG 4B0U7 17,
B3 PROUD! 0NLY
C3R741N P30PL3 C4N
R3AD 7H15.

I cdnuolt blveiee that I cluod aulaclty uesdnatnrd what I was rdanieg. The phaonmneal pweor of the hmuan mnid, aoccdrnig to rscheearch at Cmabrigde Uinervtisy, it dseno't mtaetr in what oerdr the ltteres in a word are, the olny iproamtnt tihng is that the frsit and last ltteer be in the rghit pclae. The rset can be a taotl mses and you can still raed it whotuit a pboerlm. This is bcuseaethe huamn mnid deos not raed ervey lteter by istlef, but the word as a wlohe. Azanmig huh? Yaeh and I awlyas tghuhot slpeling was ipmorantt!"

Your brain is truly an amazing piece of machinery!

John Assaraf does a lot of amazing work on how the brain actually works and how to use it to realize your dreams. He has many programs to help people better understand how their brain works and the thing they need to change in their subconscious programming to be successful with their dreams.

Neuroscientists have finally been able to Discover and explain the idea of BRAIN PLASTICITY. Now we KNOW that our brains are NOT hard-wired, but can be RE-wired and RE-trained to function in harmony with whatever your dreams may be. Some people say, "I can do this or I can't do that because my brain does not operate that way". Science has shown us that our brains are totally flexible and adjustable. If we are willing to work at it, we can change the way we think feel and perceive the world around us. This incredible discovery of how our conscious and subconscious aspects of our brain changes can be referred as Brain Plasticity.

Think of your subconscious thoughts and beliefs like a thermostat in your home. When you set a thermostat to your desired temperature, if it gets too cold, it turns on the heat to adjust it and if it gets too warm, it turns on cold air to lower the temperature. When dealing with your brain, this adjustment is called the "cybernetic mechanism". This mechanism occurs naturally in animals and has been engineered into certain machines and computerized systems. John gives an example of how the guidance missiles and thermostats both rely on these mechanisms to control, manage and constantly adjust their settings to zero in on their target.

Another example John Assaraf gives is in prehistoric times, these emotional triggers protected humans from danger, telling us if we should fight, freeze, or flee. They manipulated our internal thoughts, emotions, habits and beliefs to keep us feeling comfortable, safe and secure. You have many different internal "thermostats" to keep you in your comfort zones, and they are controlled by the emotional centers of your brain. However, today they don't always help us; in fact, they can hurt us.

Let's say you're 300 lbs overweight. You know it makes sense to eat better and exercise to get in shape. But if your brain was conditioned to keep you stuck at your current weight, stuck in your "comfort zone", you'd keep repeating the gain and loss cycle over and over and never getting ahead and staying there! Millions of people experience this in their lives today. They keep trying diet after diet. What they really need to change is how they THINK about food — and the BEHAVIORS those old thoughts and beliefs create.

Become Unconsciously Competent

In order to know your subconscious brain is operating in harmony with your dreams, you need to get to a state of subconscious competence. In this state, your mind, body and soul are operating on automatic pilot in getting to your goal of becoming rich. There are 4 stages your mind must go through to have fully functioning neurons dedicated to your end goal.

I heard Kevin Trudeau of Natural Cures break down these stages best. He said once you are at a stage of unconscious competence, your mind, body and soul will primed to get you to your success goals. This can only be achieved through unyielding repetition, constant visualization and steady positive affirmations.

Stages 1: Unconscious Incompetence

At this stage, your brain is in its infancy state. You don't know what you don't know. Not knowing there are tools readily available to get you to your goal of riches, is the state of most people. Ignorance can not only be bliss, it can be a perpetual state of mental slavery and bondage. The people in this stage feel lost and have no direction or clue on how to get out of their current economic situation. Every experience, interaction and reaction to life further confirms their state of no hope. Since we are creatures of constant expansion, naturally we will seek out answers to our external and internal questions – enter conscious incompetence.

Stages 2: Conscious Incompetence

This is the stage where we get an epiphany. We begin to look at others who are transitioning to states of increased riches and we begin to recognize we don't know the "secret sauce" to riches. This is a very critical stage. The neurons in your brain are at the cross roads. Either you will start to develop new neural pathways which align with becoming rich or your old stage of unconscious incompetence will be strengthened sending you back to a state of no hope and no way out.

I hope you will not be like the majority of people and recognize it is possible to become rich but you do not know how to do it. Once you start to seek out the answers to the questions you are asking about becoming rich. If you are reading this book, then clearly you have exited this stage and are either in the conscious incompetence or unconscious competence stage(s)

Stages 3: Conscious Competence

This is where the real mental work begins to becoming rich. You start educating yourself on how to become rich, you attempt to change your daily habits and consciously seek out methods to help you reach your end goal of riches. You know what is required to get rich.

You only master this stage by unstopping repetition of that taking the action steps required to becoming rich. Then, integrate steady visualization of you living out your dreams in the present tense, and positive affirmations of your desire of becoming rich. This is how you develop and strengthen the neural pathways required for the mindset of the rich. While you are working on your conscious competence, you should be observing someone's ability to achieve what you desire. It is as primal as monkey see, monkey do. Through studying and mimicking mentors, teachers, and living success stories doing it in real time, you will be able to benefit from their experience(s).

Stages 4: Unconscious Competence

At this stage, your brain is firing at the level of millionaire mindset. Gerry Robert has a book entitled The *Millionaire Mindset* which is another great tool to get you to this stage. Once at the unconscious competence, your brain is on auto pilot. You don't have to think about your efforts, it becomes as easy as tying your shoes. Opportunities come to you with ease and you recognize resources to help increase your riches. Your neural pathways are solidified, strong and will continue to grow as it relates to becoming rich. This stage is a testament to the power of persistence.

Working with your positive vibrations, coming into alignment with the desires that you seek is an important part because it summons the energy of the universe to help you achieve what you desire. Once your brain is in harmony with the world and you understand and believe in your rich potential, you are well on your way to becoming rich. With the power of persistence to fuel your dreams – it will happen to you. I urge even beg you to take action and be persistent with your desire to become rich.

STEP 3
CONSTRUCT YOUR MASTERMIND

Talent wins games,
but teamwork and intelligence wins championships."

Michael Jordan

THE POWER OF MENTORSHIP

"What is a teacher? I'll tell you: it isn't someone who teaches something, but someone who inspires the student to give of her best in order to discover what she already knows."

Paulo Coelho

Who needs Mentors

Mentors come in many shapes and sizes. Some mentors can be lifelong teachers and others play a specific role in your development. Regardless of how long you have a mentor, they have the power to help shape your future and even save you time and possible detours in your quest to become successful. Mentors help you to utilize your strengths and improve on your God given abilities by teaching you how to fish (develop your logic and understanding) instead of just giving you the fish (the answers).

Mentors help draw out the talent you possess and show you how to share that talent with the world. Consider this analogy - as you search for your path to riches, in the beginning it is as if you are in a room of darkness. In that room are many boxes with the different methods to create wealth for yourself. Some will usher success and some will lead you to failure. A mentor is like a flashlight who shines light in the right direction and helps you focus on where you should be looking and what areas to avoid. Mentors are your guides to help save you time and money on your journey to riches. Mentors are further down the road and can help you look out for pitfalls along the way which would you would have otherwise not been aware of.

Personal Reflections: Outside of Jesus and my parents, my first mentors were Orin Isaacs and Ivan Berry. They did not have to but took the extra time to see the potential within me. They did not consciously decide to mentor me but, instead, I gravitated toward them and naturally started picking up some of their teachings. In high school, I was a steady D student. I had no motivation to excel at anything other than sports. The problem was I did not identify my passion and, to be honest, the guidance teachers were not of any help. Guidance teachers should be semi-mentors but the ones at the time I was in high school did nothing to inspire me. It was not until my 2nd last year that I found my first mentor, Orin Isaacs. This was my first introduction to the music industry. He taught me there are many roads to making money outside of the traditional methods. He had a recording studio in the heart of downtown Toronto and I had the opportunity to see, feel and touch the benefits of his hard work. Orin took his passion for music and created a behind the scenes career out of it. It was at this point I realized the importance of hard work in whatever you do as it preps you for success in your passion.

The next year, I went from a D student to an A student. Not because I became smarter but because I identified my passion for the music industry and understood I had to work hard to work in that industry. I started hanging out more with Orin in my spare time, asking questions about the industry and what it took to win in music. Through spending time with him, I met important players at the time in Canadian music and started utilizing the teachings provided in my school work and life habits. After high school, Orin suggested I attend Harris Institute and get a diploma in Recording Arts Management. His guidance is what led me to my next important mentor, Ivan Berry.

While at Harris Institute, it was refreshing to be surrounded by students with the same interest and drive to help shape the music industry. Some of my past classmates are now in positions of influence at Universal Music, Coca Cola, and The Discovery channel. During my time at Harris, there was one class that planted a seed in my brain which grew slowly and did not produce fruit until maybe 14 years later. This class was the art of leadership led by Ivan Berry. In this class, the only way you could pass was if you came up with an original business idea (in or outside of music).

The process of using your creative faculty in the efforts for coming up with new ideas is a very important exercise. As children, we used to use our creative faculties all the time. From playing with our fingers to emulate people, to daydreaming about far off fantasy worlds, our creative faculties are what fuel all inventions, innovations and life improvements everyone on earth benefits from. I probably would not have had the privilege of being a student in this class if it were not for my first mentor Orin Isaacs (3 years prior). The Art of Leadership class also led to personally getting to know Ivan Berry (who was my second major influence in my journey to riches).

Ivan Berry at the time not only taught at Harris Institute, he also owned the first large scale Urban Music Company in Canada called BeatFactory. I watched as he took his passion to increase the exposure of Urban music at a time when it was not a popular music genre (imagine that). He taught me that very few people can identify their passion because of all the distractions of life. He also taught me that even with that small percentage of people who do identify their passion, they do not take the required steps to properly plan out a plan to achieve their goals. They are also not willing to be flexible to entertain opportunities when they present themselves – which is why many people fail.

Orin Isaacs and Ivan Berry were my first mentors who helped me realize my potential and inspired me to seek for more. The magic in mentors is I did not fully utilize these seeds for success until years later. This may be the case for you as well. Do you have someone in your life who is a mentor in disguise? Mentors come in many shapes and forms. It can be your co-worker, boss, best friend and even a stranger whom you admire. If this person provides even an ounce of inspiration or motivation, you should seek out more knowledge from them. You will be surprised the seeds they can plant in you. It may take time for these seeds to blossom but as you continue on your road to become rich, you will start to see the fruits of their input on your life. If you believe you do not have a single person in your network, you are not lost as you can seek them out. Birds of a feather flock together. If you are unable to find anyone around you to help motivate and inspire you, then it is a good indication you need to create new relationships and minimize others.

At some point, you have realize you must become a "learn it all" and avoid the "know it all". All successful and rich people have had a mentor who had assisted them. No person is an island and without the help and assistance of others, you will remain stagnant. Even in ancient times, knowledge and best practices were passed down to be utilized for the improvement of the tribe. Everyone who wants to become rich must have some form of mentor to help guide them on their road to riches.

All Superstars need Coaches

Lebron James is arguably one of the best basketball players in the world, but without proper coaching to help train, develop his abilities and basketball IQ, he would never be the icon he is today. The same training and coaching are required for anyone who wants to become rich. Being able to learn, mimic and benefit from someone who is already where you want to be is essential to help guide you on your journey to riches. A mentor does not even have to be someone you know personally; it can be someone you follow via one of their books, personal development programs or seminars. I have had and still have many different mentors who assist in keeping me on track to realize my dreams. Mentors such as Bob Proctor, Myles Munroe, Raymond Aaron, Ivan Berry, John Assaraf, Stuart Knight and a host of other amazing people have assisted me in some form or fashion in my journey to success.

As stated above, you do not have to personally know the mentor who will help you. In today's world of technology, information gathering and global markets, you just need to have the will to learn. Bob Proctor is known around the world for the work he spearheads on the law of attraction. Being a Christian, I find many of his teachings match those in the bible as well as other religious teachings. I prescribe to his teachings and follow his direction on success planning. Even after purchasing many of his mentorship programs and reading up on the knowledge he shares with the world, I have yet to meet him personally. Still, his teachings have been invaluable in my development for success.

If you are blessed enough to be around individuals who are successful, on the path to increased success or have a desire to succeed, you need to engage them and seek out their perspective on success. The best type of training is hands-on training and the best way to learn from them is to help them with their efforts. I repeat: the best way to learn from a mentor is to help them with their efforts. Through helping them, you, in turn, help yourself learn from their requests, habits and success tactics. This happens very naturally as they share their experiences with you, provide best practices on success and give you advice on your efforts as your relationship develops.

Some people have asked me, "How do I know I have the right mentor?" The answer is if the person operates with integrity, honesty and is at a place where you have yet to reach, they make a good mentor. As you develop, you may outgrow a mentor, but always look for someone who is or has been where you would like to be. You are a superstar in the making and without the guidance and direction of a coach, you will never reach your full potential. Mentors are the people in your life who will show you the path to the promised land of riches. The best time to start working with a mentor is yesterday, the second best time is today – so get started and work with a mentor to coach you to success.

Are you really ready to learn?

In 2011, I heard Kevin Trudeau speak at a seminar on "having it all" and he spoke about the power of solid mentorship as it relates to "having it all". Not only do you need mentorship to guide you to success, YOU have to play your part in the interaction. You must be ready to be taught and become the best mentee you can be. The way to do this is to be honest with yourself and with your interactions with those you look to learn from. Below are some question you should be not only asking yourself but be willing to acknowledge what you need to work on.

1. **Who do you listen to**? While you are on your journey to riches, many people will want to offer their opinion on the topic. As humans, we always have one of two choices when people give us advice: either accept or reject the information given to us. When it comes to matters of how to become rich and what it takes to become wealthy, only listen to those who are successful and rich. If you were on vacation, would you ask advice on the best place to eat from someone who has never been or experienced the desired restaurant you are looking for? Of course not. Same with advice on becoming rich. Many people will give their advice on what you should be doing, but until they can prove their theories with real riches' examples, there is no logic to suggest you should listen to them.

2. **What is your Teachability Index?** What is your willingness to learn and what is your willingness to accept change? As stated earlier in the book, some people are merely interested in becoming rich and others are dedicated to becoming rich. You must be willing to do new things and activities to have results you have never had. **Proverbs 14:23** says, *"All hard work leads to a profit but mere talk leads to poverty"*. Simply talking about what you want to do or should be doing is fine and dandy until you are committed and willing to take the action steps. The teachability index moves from 0 to 10. 0 meaning you know you know nothing and 10 meaning you know everything. As you progress with your mentor and learn new concepts and get advice on how to do things better, faster and more in alignment with the millionaire mindset, you progress to level 10. As you evolve and grow, your teachability should return back to zero even if you think you are becoming more enlightened. It is easy to feel smarter than the teacher (just look at children when they challenge the wisdom of their parents as they increase their mental capacity). Humbleness is the keep to the desire of continued learning and the understanding that humans are in a constant state of growth is also know you that there is always something to be learned.

3. **Do you know what the Training balance scale is?** Understanding the relationship between your thoughts (the what) and your techniques (the how). When learning from a mentor you should focus on *the what*. Another way put is controlling your thoughts. You are what you think and mentors help remind you what is important to you through your daily thoughts. In a given day, your end goal

of becoming rich should be to have a high frequency rate of thinking about why you want to become rich and all the good you can add to the world through your resources. Your thoughts need to match your desired end result. Many people become stagnant in achieving their desired goals by placing too much emphasis on the *how*. Do not worry about how you will get there; even though it is important, it is secondary. If you drive at night, you know the end destination but you cannot see the entire path. As you progress, the path becomes clear little by little until you finally reach your destination. Do not worry about the how, As your thoughts control your actions, following your mentors' direction will becomes easy

YOUR POOL OF WEALTH

"Empty pockets never held anyone back. Only empty heads and empty hearts can do that."

Norman Vincent Peale

Building your mastermind

Now that you have identified you passion and proceeded with your plan to riches, you have to ensure your team is set up to assist you to your end goal. This assistance comes from you delegating tasks and items which are your weaknesses, new contacts realized through introductions, advice provided to get you back on track, or even sharing your plan with those invested in your mutual successes. Another phrase for building your team is building your mastermind. Your mastermind is the collective of people in your network who will lift you on their shoulders and get you to become rich. Even though your mastermind provides great assistance to you, the main source and purpose of the mastermind is to take all the assets of each participant and create an elevated consciousness where new creative ideas are incubated to birth your riches. Your master mind comes in two parts which are **the brain** (your mentor(s) and yourself who map out your path to riches) & ***the body*** (which is your network of individuals working with you to your path to riches). Earlier in this book, I have spoken about the power and importance of mentorship; it is combination of strong mentorship and a solidified support system which will propel you to greatness.

To have a successful mastermind there must be various levels of expertise, knowledge and skills. Having a mastermind of like minded individuals is not enough to create winning results. If you want to bake a pie, you can have all the ingredients and still fail to bake a delicious cake. With the knowledge of the correct process, steps and things to watch for, which comes from a mentor or coach, you can use your ingredients (your team) to create what others will praise and enjoy in the future. A successful mastermind must (1) spark creativity, (2) assist in forward momentum, (3) have direction and vision for end results, and lastly, (4) create an atmosphere where failing is the harder option.

Your Network is your Net worth

Building your mastermind is not just about finding a mentor or coach and assembling your support system. You must be conscious of all the working parts and know what role each person (including yourself) plays in the success of your attainment of riches. Only you and your mentor or coach should know the ultimate goal. However, you must still give all the other working parts aspects of your vision to motivate, stimulate and inspire their involvement.

The Brain: When building your mastermind, the control centre is the combination of yourself and your coach or mentor. The passion, vision and end goal is the role you take and the guidance, expertise, and feedback is what your coach or mentor brings to the table.

Many coaches on success talk about the concept that your Network is your Net worth. It is another way of talking about the old time saying that *birds of a feather flock together* but with more power. Mentors help expand the network of individuals who will help you add the missing pieces to your path to riches. As your network increases, so will the opportunities which will present themselves along the way. Your job is to take your network and understand the roles they play in supercharging your efforts.

In your life, as you build up your networks, you have to be aware that different people play different roles in assisting you in achieving your goals. Some guide you to keep course, some inspire you to increase your efforts and some cheerlead you on to help motivate you. There are also people in your network who are temporary participants in your journey. They play a role for a period, then they depart from the picture (and that's alright). You have to learn to enjoy and utilize their resources while they are able to provide benefit to you. However, there are poisonous individuals who will keep you stagnant and even reverse all the hard work you invested in your goals. As the architect of your own destiny, it is up to you to be aware of all these different parts of your network. Remember, the combined parts of your network are equal to the value of your Net worth.

In a sermon on being a child of destiny, TD Jakes talks about some of these parts of your network. I will extract some of those teachings so you may apply them to your quest to become rich. TD Jakes breaks down three types of people who will come into your life and you have to be aware of them and understand the role they play in your development to become the person God intended you to be. These three types of individuals are: confidants, comrades and constituents.

Confidantes: These people for 100% for you. Whether you are up or down, confidantes are highly interested in your future success. If you have 2-3 confidants in your lifetime, you are a blessed person. These people in your network are those people who will be there for you through thick and thin. No matter how badly the situation is, they are there right beside you encouraging you to success. They have no ulterior motives to their input in your life and they only want the best for you.

This may sound like many people in your life such as a close friend or family member but that may not be the case. Many friends or family members may unintentionally look, act and sound like a confidante but a true confidante does not project their insecurities or disbeliefs towards your efforts. People in your life deep down have your best interest at heart but their paradigms can hamper your growth. A confidante is that person on the other side of success. They have done it before and want the same for you. In order for you to get to the other side of success, you need that person to show you how to scale that wall and conquer any and all adversity. A confidante feeds and fuels your goals. Actively seek out your confidante and watch the magic happen.

Constituents: Unlike a confidante who is into your success, constituents are into what you are into (not necessarily you). The distinction can be difficult at times to separate but you must develop the ability to separate the two. As long as you are progressing toward the same goals and projects as them, they will work and fight with you. You must be aware that if they come across someone else who will help further their personal efforts and agenda, they will leave you for them. If you are not careful, you will find down the road that they used your resources for their own agenda. Constituents do play a role in increasing your network and diversifying your portfolio but beware they play a role for a period of time. You will have many of these in your network and you should use them to increase your degrees of separation as you increase your net worth.

Comrades: These are the people in your network who are not for you or for your goals and projects, but they are against what you are against. These people help fight adversity and problems you may face as you have a mutual enemy (which could be lack of resources, lack of expertise and common fear of failure). They will stay with you until you have reached your common victory or project end. These people are like scaffolds used in construction. They enter into your life for a purpose and to help build your foundation. Once the project or goal has been met, just like a scaffold, they are removed – and the foundation which is your success will remain.

Don't be saddened or concerned with your comrades and constituents when they leave your network (for the benefits and new contacts you gain were worth it). Do be careful who you share your dreams with, though. Comrades and constituents are there for a time and if you share your hopes and dreams, they may take them and try to fulfill them without you. Share your mini goals but you should share your ultimate goals only with your confidantes!

3 Rules for Riches

Throughout this book, you have been given the blueprint to transform your life to one of riches, success, wealth and power. As the saying goes, with power comes great responsibility. Being rich is not only about providing a better lifestyle for those you love, it is also about being consciously aware of your responsibility to mankind. The responsibility you will have is to understand you are now part of the 3% of the population and your discretionary time and resources should help those less fortunate than you. Below are three simple rules if you want to continue to be blessed with riches.

1. **Always give back to charitable efforts:** In everyone's life, there are issues you will naturally have strong emotions and opinions for. Be it animal cruelty, humanity issues or research to find a cure for a disease. Getting involved in charitable efforts is your responsibility. Humanity is one community and when you donate your time, money and resources with no expectations but to help others, you increase your positive vibrations and the vibrations of others.

2. **Stay humble:** As someone with the ability to fulfill your desires with ease, you must remember to not brag or boast

about your blessing. Humility is the key to inviting others to continue to work with, under and around you. Remember, once you are rich, it is your responsibility to remember what it was like to be in a state of lack. To some, being rich is unrealistic but through your humility, you will be able to show people that you are the same as anyone else and if you could make it, so can they. It will also make you more approachable

3. **Be willing to mentor others:** Just as you received help along the way from a mentor, coach or guide to riches, you must continue the circle of increase. Norbord Inc. is one of the largest manufacturers of Lumber commodity. Although they distribute hundreds of truck loads worth of lumber every week, they have a very strong program to harvest and grow trees to replace what they took. The same is with you taking responsibility to harvest and grow the next "you". There is enough wealth to go around for everyone and when you allow some to learn and study from your failures and successes, you increase your foundation, and influence.

PUTTING IT ALL TOGETHER – YOU ARE READY FOR RICHES

"Most people are not going after what they want.
Even some of the most serious goal seekers and goal setters,
they're going after what they think they can get."

Bob Proctor

3 Steps to Riche$ Summary

We have come to the last chapter of 3 Steps to Riche$. I hope it has inspired you to acknowledge your worth in life and take the required steps to realizing it. Below is a summary of the 3 Steps to Riche$

1. **Identify your Passion**: Everyone in the world has a passion for something. Since it is innate to us, we may take it for granted and not attach value to it. The first step is to identify that passion and know there is a monetary equivalent to that passion. There is an industry for every passion in the world and someone is willing to pay for the value you bring to the world. Step 1 is identify your passion

2. **Map out your goals**: A dream is just a dream until you map it out; then, it becomes a goal. Take your passion and create a plan to create money and lifestyle you desire. You may have to change many aspects of your life but if your end goal is to become rich, it will be a small trade off. Step 2 is to map out your goals.

3. **Construct your mastermind**: Take you plan and build a team to help make your dreams and goals a reality. Find a mentor, increase your network and watch your dreams become a reality. Step 3 is to construct your mastermind

9 Amazing tools for success

I have created a list of some of the teachings from various mentors on habits you must develop and master if you are to become rich. I will not go into too much detail in this book but implementing any or all of these 9 tools will help makes your goals and planning for riches so much easier. These daily habits are tools which may take some time to develop but are very important in your steps to riches.

1. **Start every day before sunrise:** It was not a mistake when your parents said, "Early to bed, early to rise makes you healthy, wealthy and wise". You will be surprised at the number of extra tasks you can do when you get up earlier than you have to. To make getting up earlier, aim for extra hours of sleep. Your body is an amazing machine and needs to a good recharge every night.

2. **Surround yourself with those you wish to be like**: Like it or not, we are products of our environment. "If you want to know who you are, show me your friends". As I said earlier, birds of a feather flock together. Surrounding yourself with those you wish to be like does not even have to be physical. It can be dedicating your time to prescribing to classes, seminars and books of those with minds like yours. Step outside your comfort zone.

3. **Plan the work, then work the plan:** Plan your efforts with the end goal in mind. Plan it, write it down and map out your plan, rather than willy-nilly forward movement. Most importantly, remain flexible, because life is not stagnant. And change is good.

4. **Treat yourself to a mini getaway weekly:** Spend 15 minutes daily, meditating, relaxing and focusing on your goals and dreams. Do this in silence and, if possible, in the dark. Also get 1 hour of complete peace every weekend via a nap or continued meditation and rest.

5. **Money is a tool to be used not saved:** Money is not wealth; money is a tool to fulfill your desires. Put money to work via giving it away to the needy or have it work for you to build more wealth for yourself and those you care about.
6. **Never Stop Learning**: Read every day and continue to improve yourself. Someone said, "Your real education begins after school, not in school." If you are not growing, you are dying. Learning is the fuel of growth, and growth is necessary for success.
7. **Stay Motivated**: Inspire yourself by creating a vision board or listening to a motivational speech. Keep your energy high and spend time day dreaming of how life will be when you achieve your goals.
8. **Do a good deed every day**: Without seeking any thanks or reward, do something nice for someone EVERYDAY. It could be as small as a smile to a random stranger or words of encouragement to a loved one. Become an asset to those around you - the greater the success you want in your life, the more of an asset you must be, to as many people every day.
9. **Don't' talk about it, be about it:** Never tell people what you would like to do. Only talk about what you are doing or what you have accomplished. Many people say they will start something, but until you actually start it, shut up.

You are now ready to implement all your pools of wealth and live the life you deserve. This book provided 3 simple steps to riches but you still have to do the work required. Without you taking action, there will be no result. The wonderful thing about starting is you do not have to get off to a 100 meter dash pace. Sometimes slow and steady will also get you there – But you must start to take action. I said it before and I will say it again. Action puts flesh to faith; so if you believe you are worthy of greatness, take action and make it a reality.

Make a decision to become rich

Throughout this book, you have been provided with the tools to become rich. It starts by acknowledging you are worthy to become rich and your resources will be used for the betterment of those you love and care for. Then, you have to identify your passion which will be the vehicle to success. Once you know your industry, you have to map out your plan to get there, understanding you will have to alter your lifestyle to accommodate the growth. Lastly, you have to ensure you build a team to help you along your journey as no person is an island. Even with all these time tested tools, unless you make the decision to become rich and take the steps to get there, you will never achieve your goal. Make a decision right now to become rich, write it down and read it every day with conviction you will achieve your goal of becoming rich.

The proxy of your development will be evident from the feedback you get from the world around you. Dr. Carole N. Hildebrand said your decision must be a committed decision. Do you want to become rich (a nice to have or preference) or are you committed to becoming rich (a necessity). This is very true as a committed decision implies you will not be swayed in your efforts. The word decision comes from the Latin roots, *de*, meaning from and *caedere*, meaning to cut so in essence, a decision means cutting off all other possibilities. Are you ready to cut all options other than becoming rich? If yes, do so now.

So how do you know if you committed to your decision to become rich? Committed decisions usually show up in two places of your life:

your calendar and your chequebook. It does not matter what you think your priorities are and dedicated to becoming rich. The real proxy of your commitment to becoming rich is evident in what is in your daily calendar and the disbursements of your bank.

If you are committed to becoming rich, your calendar should be filled with reminders of educational classes on your passion, seminars on helping you attain your goals and meetings with like minded individuals who will assist you in your efforts to success. If you are not looking to increase the time you spend attaining your riches, it will not come. You must sacrifice little luxuries to attain masses of wealth. Try turning off the TV, read a self help book instead of a magazine or go to a workshop before or after work. Saying you do not have time is not an excuse. We make time for anything we have a passion for. If I said I had $1 million dollars I wanted to give you but all you had to do was sit in a room and listen to speech for 3 hours, I bet you would find a way to attend. If you are truly committed to becoming rich, your answer will be evident in your daily calendar.

Earlier in the book, I said you have to be willing to educate yourself and be open to continuous learning. Some of this continuous learning can be acquired for free but some of it requires you to spend some money. If you could make $1million dollars tomorrow, how much are you willing to spend today in order to get it? This is where many people stop moving forward to their riches. They stop treating money as a tool and look at it as their master. I am not saying you should be willing to refinance your house or use your life's saving. I am, however, saying you should be putting away a certain percentage (5-10%) for education and investing in your future. Your chequebook needs to be documented proof you are committed to becoming rich. Purchase a self help book, purchase an online class, join an investment club and pool your money for real estate. Spend your money with a cheerful heart and watch your returns come back in the way of knowledge, expertise and process to acquire more money and resources.

Becoming rich starts when you make a conscious effort to take your God given talents or passions and focusing your efforts towards a single plan. This plan should have the mandate to transform it into some sort of monetary reward for sharing with the world. The way in which you share it with the world is through creating and increasing your network with the guidance of some form of mentorship program. Becoming rich will allow you to help those in need, increase the time you spend with loved ones and ultimately create a better lifestyle for those around you.

I will end this book with a recap to a story which I hear from time to time. There was a well-known speaker who started his conference by holding up a $100.00 bill. Then, he asked the audience in the room who wanted the $100 bill? Hands started going up. Then, he said, "Would you still want it if I crumple it up?" Hands were still up. So he asked,"What if I stepped all over it with my shoe?" Then, he proceeded to do so. Even still hands were up wanting the now dirty and crumbled $100. The speaker then paused for a moment and said, "There is an important lesson to learn from this exercise". You see no matter what the speaker did to the money, still everyone wanted it because it did not decrease in value. No matter the state, it was still worth $100.

In your everyday lives, negative things happen to you. You are dropped, crumpled, grounded into the dirt and kicked around by the decisions (and indecisions) you make. At times, you may feel worthless or inefficient but no matter the situation or circumstance, you will never lose your value. Clean, dirty, crumpled, messed or polished, you are blessed and highly favored. Your value will never diminish.

The sooner you realize your true value, the faster and easier it will be to become rich. Your worth is not in how you or others perceive you. Your worth comes from knowing you are a child of the most high and special. Even if you do not believe in a higher power, there were over a million options that could have been. Out of millions of sperm - you were selected: you are 1 in a million. Don't EVER forget it.' Count your blessings, not your problems. Enjoy your journey to riches - it is as easy as 3 steps

TOOLS FOR SUCCESS

"Create a definite plan for carrying out your desire
and begin at once, whether you're ready or not,
to put this plan into action."

Napoleon Hill

POOL OF WEALTH OFFERS

Go to www.3stepstoriches.com and under the **Tools for Success** tab, you will find programs which have helped shape my path to riches and I highly recommend them for you.

As my way of saying thank you for reading this book, under **Free Resources**, you will find free videos, downloads and other documents to assist you on your path to riches (valued at $197)

Lastly, be sure to sign up for my FREE daily motivational quotes at www.poolofwealth.com